Interactive Homework Workbook

Grade 4

Scott Foresman·Addison Wesley
enVisionMATH™

Scott Foresman
is an imprint of

pearsonschool.com

Editorial Offices: Glenview, Illinois • Parsippany, New Jersey • New York, New York
Sales Offices: Boston, Massachusetts • Duluth, Georgia • Glenview, Illinois
Coppell, Texas • Sacramento, California • Mesa, Arizona

ISBN – 13: 978-0-328-34177-1

ISBN – 10: 0-328-34177-0

7 8 9 10 V004 12 11 10

Contents

Contents

Thousands

Write each number in standard form.

1. 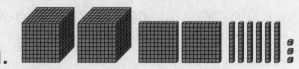   _____

2. 8 ten thousands + 4 thousands +
   9 hundreds + 4 tens + 7 ones   _____

Write the word form and tell the value of the underlined digit for
each number.

3. 7<u>6</u>,239 _____

   _____

4. 823,<u>7</u>74 _____

   _____

5. **Number Sense** Write the number that has 652 in
   the ones period and 739 in the thousands period. _____

During a weekend at the Movie Palace Theaters, 24,875 tickets
were sold. Add the following to the number of tickets sold.

6. 100 tickets _____   **7.** 1,000 tickets _____

8. Which of the following numbers has a 5 in the
   ten thousands place?

   A 652,341   **B** 562,341   **C** 462,541   **D** 265,401

9. **Writing to Explain** Explain how you know the 6 in the number 364,021 is
   NOT in the thousands place.

   _____

   _____

Millions

Write the number in standard form and in word form.

1. 300,000,000 + 70,000,000 + 2,000,000 + 500,000 + 10,000 + 2,000 + 800 + 5

_____

_____

_____

Write the word form and tell the value of the underlined digit for each number.

2. 4,<u>6</u>00,028 _____

_____

3. 488,423,0<u>4</u>6 _____

_____

4. **Number Sense** Write the number that is
one hundred million more than 15,146,481. _____

5. The population of Peru in 2006 was estimated to be 28,302,603. Write the
word form.

_____

_____

6. Which is the expanded form for 43,287,005?

   A 4,000,000 + 300,000 + 20,000 + 8,000 + 700 + 5

   B 40,000,000 + 3,000,000 + 200,000 + 80,000 + 7,000 + 5

   C 400,000,000 + 30,000,000 + 2,000,000 + 8,000 + 500

   D 4,000,000 + 30,000 + 2,000 + 800 + 70 + 5

7. **Writing to Explain** In the number 463,211,889, which digit has the
greatest value? Explain.

_____

_____

Comparing and Ordering Whole Numbers

Compare. Write > or < for each ◯ .

1. 2,854,376 ◯ 2,845,763

2. 6,789 ◯ 9,876

3. 59,635 ◯ 59,536

4. 29,374,125 ◯ 30,743,225

Order the numbers from least to greatest.

5. 45,859,211   4,936,211   43,958,211

_____   _____   _____

6. Number Sense Write three numbers that are greater than 1,543,000 but less than 1,544,000.

_____   _____   _____

7. Put the planets in order from the one closest to the sun to the one farthest from the sun.

_____

_____

_____

_____

The Five Closest Planets to the Sun

Planet	Distance (miles)
Earth	93,000,000
Jupiter	483,000,000
Mars	142,000,000
Mercury	36,000,000
Venus	67,000,000

8. Which number has the greatest value?

A 86,543,712   **B** 82,691,111   **C** 85,381,211   **D** 86,239,121

9. Writing to Explain Tell how you could use a number line to determine which of two numbers is greater.

_____

_____

Rounding Whole Numbers

Round each number to the nearest ten.

1. 16,326   **2.** 412,825   **3.** 6,512,162   **4.** 42,084,097

_____   _____   _____   _____

Round each number to the nearest hundred.

5. 1,427   **6.** 68,136   **7.** 271,308   **8.** 7,593,656

_____   _____   _____   _____

Round each number to the nearest thousand.

9. 18,366   **10.** 409,614   **11.** 48,229,930   **12.** 694,563,239

_____   _____   _____   _____

Round each number to the underlined place.

13. 12,108   **14.** 570,274   **15.** 9,333,625   **16.** 534,307,164

_____   _____   _____   _____

17. What is 681,542 rounded to the nearest hundred thousand?

A 600,000   **B** 680,000   **C** 700,000   **D** 780,000

18. **Writing to Explain** Mrs. Kennedy is buying pencils for each
of 315 students at Hamilton Elementary. The pencils are sold
in boxes of tens. How can she use rounding to decide how
many pencils to buy?

_____

_____

_____

Using Money to Understand Decimals

1. 2.18 = _____ ones + _____ tenth + _____ hundredths

   $2.18 = _____ dollars + _____ dime + _____ pennies

2. 9.27 = _____ ones + _____ hundredths

   $9.27 = _____ dollars + _____ pennies

3. 7.39 = _____ ones + _____ tenths + _____ hundredths

   $7.39 = _____ dollars + _____ dimes + _____ pennies

4. **Number Sense** Write 3 dollars, 9 dimes, and 5 pennies with a dollar sign and decimal point.

   _____

5. **Number Sense** If you have 5 tenths of a dollar, how much money do you have?

   _____

6. Lana wants to buy a book for $6.95. How can she pay for the book using only dollars, dimes, and nickels?

   _____

7. How would you write sixteen and twenty-five hundredths with a decimal point?

   A 16.025   **B** 16.25   **C** 162.5   **D** 1,625

8. **Writing to Explain** Which is greater, 4 tenths and 2 hundredths or 2 tenths and 4 hundredths? Explain.

   _____

   _____

   _____

Name _____

Counting Money and Making Change

For Exercises **1** through **8**, find the change from a $10 bill.

1. $6.35 _____   **2.** $1.28 _____   **3.** $9.01 _____   **4.** $3.11 _____

5. $8.88 _____   **6.** $7.70 _____   **7.** $0.37 _____   **8.** $4.56 _____

For Exercises **9** through **12**, find each amount of money.

9. _____   **10.** _____   **11.** _____   **12.** _____

13. Veronica buys a dress for $45.99. She can pay with a $50 bill. What is the amount of money Veronica received in change?

_____

14. Linda spent $6.64, including tax, on a pair of socks. She paid with a $10 bill. What is the fewest number of coins that she might get back in change?

A 3   **B** 5   **C** 8   **D** 9

15. Writing to Explain Mike's bill for stamps comes out to $19.35. He paid with a $20 bill. He got 8 coins back as change. Is this possible? Explain.

_____

_____

Problem Solving:
Make an Organized List

Make an organized list to solve each problem. Write each
answer in a complete sentence.

1. Tonya and Lauren are designing a soccer uniform. They
want to use two colors on the shirt. Their choices are
green, orange, yellow, purple, blue, and silver. How many
ways can they choose two colors?

_____

_____

_____

2. Yancey collects plastic banks. He has three different banks:
a pig, a cow, and a horse. How many ways can Yancey
arrange his banks on a shelf?

_____

_____

3. Kevin has a rabbit, a ferret, a gerbil, and a turtle. He feeds
them in a different order each day. In how many different
orders can Kevin feed his pets?

_____

_____

_____

_____

Using Mental Math to Add and Subtract

Add or subtract. Use mental math.

1. 89 + 46

2. 101 − 49

3. 400 + 157

_____

_____

_____

4. 722 + 158

5. 120 − 33

6. 900 − 187

_____

_____

_____

7. 299 + 206

8. 878 + 534

9. 554 − 59

_____

_____

_____

10. **Reasoning** How can you write
52 + (8 + 25) to make it easier to add? _____

11. Selena's family went on a trip. The total hotel bill was $659.
The cost of the airfare was $633. Use mental math to find the
total cost for the hotel and the airfare. _____

12. One year, 76 people helped at the town cleanup. The next
year, 302 people helped. How many more people helped in
the second year? Use mental math to find the answer. _____

13. Stanley wants to collect 900 sports cards. So far, he has
collected 428 baseball cards and 217 football cards. How
many more cards does Stanley need to complete his
collection?

A 255

B 472

C 645

D 683

14. **Writing to Explain** Explain how you could add 678 + 303
using mental math.

_____

_____

Estimating Sums and Differences of Whole Numbers

Estimate each sum or difference.

1. 627
 $+\ \ 95$

2. 829
 $-\ 292$

3. 987
 $-\ 233$

4. 1,568
 $+\ \ 352$

5. $4,263 - 1,613$ _____

6. $7,502 + 2,187$ _____

7. $24,141 - 2,177$

8. $64,099 - 55,555$

9. $83,595 + 18,999$

_____ _____ _____

10. About how much larger is the largest
 ocean than the smallest ocean?

_____

_____

Ocean Area

Ocean	Area (million sq km)
Arctic Ocean	14,056
Atlantic Ocean	76,762
Indian Ocean	68,556
Pacific Ocean	155,557

11. About how many million square kilometers do all the oceans
 together cover?

_____

12. Mallory is a pilot. Last week she flew the following round trips
 in miles: 2,020; 1,358; 952; 2,258; and 1,888. Which of the
 following is a good estimate of the miles Mallory flew last week?

 A 6,000 mi **B** 6,800 mi **C** 7,000 mi **D** 8,000 mi

13. **Writing to Explain** Explain how you would estimate to
 subtract 189 from 643.

_____

_____

Problem Solving:
Missing or Extra Information

For **1** through **3**, decide if each problem has extra information or not enough information. Tell any information that is not needed or that is missing. Solve if you have enough information.

1. Kendall pitches for his school's baseball team. Every game Kendall pitches, he averages 5 strikeouts per game. Each game is about 2 hours. If Kendall pitches in 7 games during the season, how many strikeouts will he have?

_____

2. **Geometry** Yolanda is putting up a fence for her dog in the shape of a square. Each foot of fencing costs $7. If Yolanda is planning to have each side of the fence be 10 feet long, how many feet of fencing will Yolanda need?

_____

3. Gretchen sings and plays guitar in a band after school. If Gretchen sings half of the songs the band knows, how many songs does the band know?

_____

4. What do you need to know if you're trying to find the year George Washington was born and you know he died in 1799?

   A The current year   C How old he was when he died

   B The exact date he died   D There is enough information.

5. **Writing to Explain** If you wanted to write a word problem about how much money the fourth-grade class collected at their bake sale, what information would you need to include?

_____

Adding Whole Numbers

Add.

1.	2.	3.	4.
486	4,334	938	7,226
875	4,948	1,487	1,587
+ 45	+ 890	+ 8,947	+ 72,984

5.	6.	7.	8.
	80	27,987	8,738
54,236	960	2,096	5,234
223	4	15,098	836
+ 7,856	+ 1,986	+ 7,945	+ 237

9. **Number Sense** Luke added 429 + 699 + 314 and got 950.
Is this sum reasonable?

_____

10. What is the combined
length of the three
longest glaciers?

_____

11. What is the total
combined length of
the four longest
glaciers in the world?

World's Longest Glaciers

Glacier	Length (miles)
Lambert-Fisher Ice Passage	320
Novaya Zemlya	260
Arctic Institute Ice Passage	225
Nimrod-Lennox-King	180

_____

12. Which is the sum of 3,774 + 8,276 + 102?

A 1,251　　　**B** 12,152　　　**C** 13,052　　　**D** 102,152

13. **Writing to Explain** Leona added 6,641 + 1,482 + 9,879.
Should her answer be more than or less than 15,000?

_____

Subtracting Whole Numbers

Subtract.

1. 7,242
   − 158

2. 520
   − 203

3. 848
   − 257

4. 6,797
   − 1,298

5. 753
   − 218

6. 7,392
   − 4,597

7. 3,898
   − 1,299

8. 3,721
   − 459

9. 3,328 − 1,754   **10.** 9,333 − 1,555   **11.** 6,797 − 1,298

12. Which of the following best describes the answer to the
subtraction problem below?

   3,775 − 1,831

   A The answer is less than 1,000.

   B The answer is about 1,000.

   C The answer is greater than 1,000.

   D You cannot tell from the information given.

13. **Writing to Explain** The Environmental Club's goal is to
collect 1,525 cans by the end of the summer. The number of
cans they collected each week is shown in the table below.
How can you find the number of cans they need to collect in
week 4 to meet their goal?

Week Number	Number of cans collected
1	378
2	521
3	339
4	

_____

_____

Subtracting Across Zeros

Subtract.

1. $\begin{array}{r} 906 \\ -\ \ 45 \\ \hline \end{array}$

2. $\begin{array}{r} 3,091 \\ -\ 1,361 \\ \hline \end{array}$

3. $\begin{array}{r} 4,000 \\ -\ 2,557 \\ \hline \end{array}$

4. $\begin{array}{r} 800 \\ -\ 139 \\ \hline \end{array}$

5. $\begin{array}{r} 1,070 \\ -\ \ 593 \\ \hline \end{array}$

6. $\begin{array}{r} 8,904 \\ -\ 3,596 \\ \hline \end{array}$

7. $\begin{array}{r} 3,007 \\ -\ 2,366 \\ \hline \end{array}$

8. $\begin{array}{r} 523 \\ -\ 203 \\ \hline \end{array}$

9. $7,403 - 3,254$

10. $5,067 - 2,987$

11. $6,790 - 1,298$

_____   _____   _____

12. Robert set a goal to swim 1,000 laps in the local
swimming pool during his summer break. Robert has
currently finished 642 laps. How many more laps
does he have to swim in order to meet his goal?

A 332   **B** 358   **C** 468   **D** 472

13. **Writing to Explain** If $694 - 72 =$ _____, then $622 +$ _____ $= 694$.
Explain the process of checking your work.

_____

_____

_____

_____

Problem Solving: Draw a Picture and Write an Equation

For exercises **1** through **4** write an equation and solve. Use the picture to help you.

1. A remote control car has a speed of 5 feet per second. How many feet will the car travel in 6 seconds?

_____

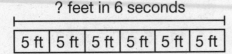

? feet in 6 seconds

| 5 ft | 5 ft | 5 ft | 5 ft | 5 ft | 5 ft |

2. Danny has 45 minutes to take a math test. If Danny finishes half the test in 19 minutes, how many minutes does he have left to finish it?

45 minutes

| 19 minutes | ? minutes left |

3. While shopping, Janet bought a shirt for $8, a pair of jeans for $22, mittens for $5, and a hat for $10. How much money did Janet spend?

_____

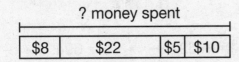

? money spent

| $8 | $22 | $5 | $10 |

4. The 175th anniversary of the completion of the Erie Canal was in the year 2000. If it took 8 years to dig the canal, in what year did the digging of the Erie Canal begin?

_____

Year 2000

| 175 | 8 | ? year digging began |

5. The average length of a song on a certain CD is 3 minutes. The CD has 12 songs. Write an equation for the length of the whole CD. Draw a picture to help you.

A 12×3 **B** $12 + 3$ **C** $12 \div 3$ **D** $12 - 3$

6. Writing to Explain It takes Jinny 56 minutes to drive to her friend's house. She drove 15 minutes and then stopped at a store. She then drove another 10 minutes. What do you need to do to find the amount of time she has left to drive?

_____

_____

_____

Meanings of Multiplication

Write an addition sentence and a multiplication sentence for the picture.

1.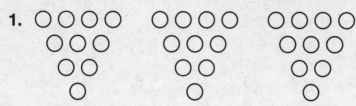

_____

Write a multiplication sentence for each addition sentence.

2. $4 + 4 + 4 + 4 = 16$ _____

3. $10 + 10 + 10 + 10 + 10 + 10 = 60$ _____

4. Number Sense How could you use multiplication to find $7 + 7 + 7$?

_____

5. A classroom desk has 4 legs. How many legs do
5 desks have altogether? _____

6. Danielle planted 3 seeds in 6 different pots.
How many seeds did she plant? _____

7. Which is the multiplication sentence for $2 + 2 + 2 + 2$?

A $4 \times 4 = 16$ **B** $2 \times 2 = 4$ **C** $4 \times 2 = 8$ **D** $2 \times 6 = 12$

8. Writing to Explain Explain how you can use multiplication
to find $2 + 2 + 2 + 2$.

_____

_____

_____

Patterns for Facts

1. 5
    $\times\ 4$

2. 2
    $\times\ 3$

3. 9
    $\times\ 7$

4. 5
    $\times\ 2$

5. 8
    $\times\ 2$

6. 5
    $\times\ 3$

7. 9
    $\times\ 8$

8. 9
    $\times\ 4$

9. $9 \times 6 =$ _____

10. $2 \times 7 =$ _____

11. $5 \times 5 =$ _____

Algebra Find the missing number.

12. _____ $\times\ 9 = 45$

13. $2 \times$ _____ $= 14$

14. A package of baseball cards includes 5 cards. How many baseball cards are in 5 packages?

_____

15. What is the value of the missing number?
     $9 \times \boxed{} = 36$

     A 6   **B** 4   **C** 3   **D** 2

16. **Writing to Explain** Milton needs to find the product of two numbers. One of the numbers is 9. The answer also needs to be 9. How will he solve this problem? Explain.

_____

_____

_____

Multiplication Properties

1.
$$\begin{array}{r} 0 \\ \times\ 4 \\ \hline \end{array}$$

2.
$$\begin{array}{r} 1 \\ \times\ 3 \\ \hline \end{array}$$

3.
$$\begin{array}{r} 7 \\ \times\ 1 \\ \hline \end{array}$$

4.
$$\begin{array}{r} 5 \\ \times\ 0 \\ \hline \end{array}$$

5.
$$\begin{array}{r} 1 \\ \times\ 8 \\ \hline \end{array}$$

6.
$$\begin{array}{r} 3 \\ \times\ 0 \\ \hline \end{array}$$

7.
$$\begin{array}{r} 4 \\ \times\ 1 \\ \hline \end{array}$$

8.
$$\begin{array}{r} 6 \\ \times\ 0 \\ \hline \end{array}$$

9. $1 \times 1 =$ _____

10. $9 \times 0 =$ _____

11. $0 \times 0 =$ _____

Algebra Find the missing number.

12. _____ $\times 9 = 0$

13. $1 \times$ _____ $= 4$

14. Ray has 4 boxes with 5 pens in each box. Kevin has 5 boxes with 4 pens in each. Who has more pens?

_____

15. Which property can help you find the missing number? _____ $\times 9 = 0$

_____

16. **Writing to Explain** Steve needs to find the product of two numbers. One of the numbers is 6. The answer also needs to be 6. How will you solve this problem? Explain.

_____

_____

_____

3 and 4 as Factors

Use breaking apart to find each product.

1. $\begin{array}{r} 3 \\ \times\ 7 \\ \hline \end{array}$ 2. $\begin{array}{r} 4 \\ \times\ 9 \\ \hline \end{array}$ 3. $\begin{array}{r} 3 \\ \times\ 4 \\ \hline \end{array}$ 4. $\begin{array}{r} 4 \\ \times\ 6 \\ \hline \end{array}$

5. $4 \times 5 =$ _____   6. $3 \times 9 =$ _____   7. $3 \times 5 =$ _____

8. $3 \times 6 =$ _____   9. $4 \times 7 =$ _____   10. $3 \times 8 =$ _____

11. **Number Sense** Sara traced circle stencils for her project. She needs 4 rows of 6 circle stencils. She thought that 4 rows of 6 is the same as 3 rows of 8 and 2 rows of 8. Is this correct? Explain.

_____

_____

_____

12. Which of the following is equal to the product of 3×3?

   A 9×1 **B** 3×1 **C** 4×2 **D** 6×3

13. **Writing to Explain** Explain how the three multiplication sentences are related.

   2×12 3×8 4×6

_____

_____

6, 7, and 8 as Factors

Use breaking apart to find each product.

1. $\begin{array}{r} 7 \\ \times\ 3 \\ \hline \end{array}$ **2.** $\begin{array}{r} 8 \\ \times\ 5 \\ \hline \end{array}$ **3.** $\begin{array}{r} 8 \\ \times\ 2 \\ \hline \end{array}$ **4.** $\begin{array}{r} 6 \\ \times\ 4 \\ \hline \end{array}$

5. $6 \times 3 =$ _____   **6.** $8 \times 3 =$ _____   **7.** $7 \times 5 =$ _____

8. $6 \times 6 =$ _____   **9.** $6 \times 7 =$ _____   **10.** $7 \times 9 =$ _____

11. **Number Sense** Meghan planted seeds for her project.
She needs 7 rows of 9 seeds. She thought that
7 rows of 9 is the same as 3 rows of 9 and 2 rows of 9.
Is this correct?

_____

_____

_____

_____

12. Which of the following is equal to the product of 8×3?

A 7×4 **B** 6×4 **C** 6×2 **D** 8×2

13. **Writing to Explain** Explain how the three multiplication
sentences are related.
6×2 4×3 12×1

_____

10, 11, and 12 as Factors

1. $4 \times 10 =$ _____   **2.** $12 \times 2 =$ _____   **3.** $10 \times 6 =$ _____

4. $11 \times 1 =$ _____   **5.** $4 \times 12 =$ _____   **6.** $8 \times 11 =$ _____

7. $9 \times 10 =$ _____   **8.** $12 \times 3 =$ _____   **9.** $10 \times 7 =$ _____

10. $11 \times 5 =$ _____   **11.** $10 \times 5 =$ _____   **12.** $6 \times 12 =$ _____

13. **Number Sense** Beatrice multiplied 10×9. She quickly found the answer by placing a 0 behind the 9 to get an answer of 90. Is this reasonable?

_____

_____

There are 12 months in 1 year. How many months are in

14. 2 years? _____

15. 3 years? _____

16. 5 years? _____

17. In the classroom there are 5 round tables. There are 4 students sitting at each table. How many students are sitting at the tables altogether? _____

18. How much money is 12 dimes?

    A $0.60   **B** $1.00   **C** $1.20   **D** $2.00

19. **Writing to Explain** Explain how to find 7×11.

_____

_____

_____

Problem Solving: Draw a Picture and Write an Equation

For **1** through **4**, write an equation and solve. Use the picture to help.

1. John is running in a marathon. The marathon is 25 miles long. After two hours, John has run 7 miles. How many miles does John have left to run?

_____

25 miles

7	? miles

2. A summer camp has divided its campers into 4 groups of 25 campers. How many campers are at the summer camp?

_____

? campers

25	25	25	25

3. Karen is 5 feet tall. In Karen's backyard there is an oak tree 4 times as tall as she is. How tall is the oak tree?

_____

? feet

Oak tree | 5 ft | 5 ft | 5 ft | 5 ft |

Karen | 5 ft |

4. Micah's room has four sides and a perimeter of 48 feet. If 3 of the sides are 12 feet long, how long is the fourth side?

_____

48 feet

12 ft	12 ft	12 ft	?

5. On Monday, Chris had $250 in his savings account. On Friday, he spent $16 at the movies. On Saturday, he deposited a $120 check. Which number sentence below shows how much money Chris has?

A 250 + 16 + 120

B 250 + 16 − 120

C 250 − 16 − 120

D 250 − 16 + 120

6. Writing to Explain Melissa is making bookmarks from a piece of ribbon that is 12 inches long. Each bookmark is 4 inches long. She drew this picture to see how many bookmarks she could make from the ribbon. What did she do wrong?

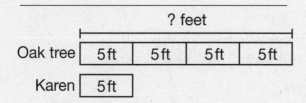

12 in. in all

4 inches	4 inches	4 inches	4 inches

Meanings of Division

Draw pictures to solve each problem.

1. There are 12 small gift bags. Each bag can hold 1 toy and some stickers. There are 36 stickers. If an equal number of stickers is put in each bag, how many stickers will be in each bag?

_____

2. One egg carton holds 12 eggs. How many cartons are you able to fill with 60 eggs?

_____

3. There are 21 students in Mr. Tentler's class. The students divided themselves evenly into 3 groups. How many students are in each group? _____

4. Calvin read an 18-page chapter in his social studies book in 2 hours. If he read the same number of pages each hour, how many pages did he read per hour?

   A 3 pages   **B** 6 pages   **C** 9 pages   **D** 12 pages

5. **Writing to Explain** The class is planning a party. The pizza restaurant cuts each pizza into 8 slices. There are 32 students. How many pizzas does the class need to order for each student to have one slice? Explain.

_____

_____

_____

Relating Multiplication and Division

Complete each fact family.

1. $7 \times$ _____ $= 42$

_____ $\times$ _____ $= 42$

$42 \div 6 =$ _____

$42 \div$ _____ $=$ _____

2. $9 \times$ _____ $= 36$

_____ $\times$ _____ $= 36$

$36 \div 4 =$ _____

$36 \div$ _____ $=$ _____

Write a fact family for each set of numbers.

3. 6, 3, 18

_____

4. 5, 5, 25

_____

5. **Reasoning** Why does the fact family for 81 and 9 have only two number sentences?

_____

_____

_____

6. Which number sentence completes the fact family?

$9 \times 6 = 54$ $54 \div 9 = 6$ $54 \div 6 = 9$

A $9 \times 9 = 81$ **B** $6 \times 9 = 54$ **C** $6 \times 6 = 36$ **D** $8 \times 6 = 48$

7. **Writing to Explain** Find two ways to divide 16 evenly. Explain.

_____

_____

Special Quotients

1. $0 \div 10 =$ _____
2. $7 \div 1 =$ _____
3. $8 \div 8 =$ _____

4. $9 \div 9 =$ _____
5. $0 \div 5 =$ _____
6. $5 \div 1 =$ _____

7. $1\overline{)4}$ _____
8. $8\overline{)0}$ _____
9. $3\overline{)3}$ _____
10. $1\overline{)6}$ _____

11. **Number Sense** If $x \div 9 = 1$, how do you know what x is? Explain.

_____

_____

12. Kenneth has 22 math problems to do for homework. He
    has 12 problems done. How many more problems does
    he have left? If he completes 1 problem every minute, how
    many more minutes does he have to work?

_____

13. There are 8 people who would like to share a box of
    granola bars that contains 8 bars. How many granola bars
    does each person get if they share equally?

_____

14. Which is the quotient of $20 \div 20$?

    A 20   **B** 2   **C** 1   **D** 0

15. **Writing to Explain** Write a rule for the following number
    sentence: $0 \div 7 = 0$.

_____

_____

_____

_____

Using Multiplication Facts to Find Division Facts

Solve.

1. $12 \div 3 =$ _____

2. $20 \div 5 =$ _____

3. $50 \div 10 =$ _____

4. $27 \div 9 =$ _____

5. $6 \div 2 =$ _____

6. $16 \div 8 =$ _____

7. $63 \div 9 =$ _____

8. $36 \div 4 =$ _____

9. $48 \div 6 =$ _____

10. $32 \div 8 =$ _____

11. $25 \div 5 =$ _____

12. $18 \div 2 =$ _____

Use the data in the table to write a multiplication story for the number fact. Solve.

13. $2 \times 6 =$

First Aid Kit	
Supply	**Number in Kit**
Bandages	4
Cleanser Pads	6
Cotton Balls	12

_____

_____

_____

14. Which is the quotient of $28 \div 7$?

A 14   **B** 9   **C** 6   **D** 4

15. Writing to Explain Write a division story for 12 and 3.

_____

_____

Problem Solving: Draw a Picture and Write an Equation

1. Terrence has 16 trophies and he wants to put an equal number on 4 shelves. How many trophies will he have on each shelf?

_____

2. Jody is making a sculpture of her dog. If the sculpture is 6 inches long and her dog is 7 times as long as the sculpture, how long is Jody's dog?

_____

3. Lisa has 45 megabytes of space left on her flash drive. She has 5 files that are the same size that will fill up the space. How many megabytes is each file?

_____

4. A store is displaying boxes of a new video game in 7 rows. If the store has 49 copies of the game how many games are in each row?

_____

5. Mrs. Lopez is 54 and has a daughter who is six years more than a third of her age. Draw a picture to help find which expression below shows how old Mrs. Lopez's daughter is.

A $54 + 6 \div 3$ **B** $54 \div 3 + 6$ **C** $54 \div 6 + 3$ **D** $54 + 3 \div 6$

6. Writing to Explain Jillian wants to organize her CD collection into wooden crates. Each crate holds 8 CDs. Jillian has 48 CDs. How can she use a picture to figure out how many crates she needs?

_____

_____

_____

Multiplying by Multiples of 10 and 100

Find each product. Use mental math.

1. $6 \times 70 =$ _____

2. $80 \times 2 =$ _____

3. $40 \times 9 =$ _____

4. $10 \times 3 =$ _____

5. $4 \times 500 =$ _____

6. $300 \times 9 =$ _____

7. $8 \times 600 =$ _____

8. $7 \times 400 =$ _____

9. $6 \times 200 =$ _____

10. $800 \times 5 =$ _____

11. $6 \times 800 =$ _____

12. $400 \times 3 =$ _____

13. Number Sense How many zeros will the product of 7×500 have? _____

Mr. Young has 30 times as many pencils as Jack. The whole school has 200 times as many pencils as Jack. If Jack has 2 pencils, how many pencils does

14. Mr. Young have?

15. the whole school have?

_____   _____

16. Find 3×100.

A 30   **B** 300   **C** 3,000   **D** 30,000

17. Writing to Explain Wendi says that the product of 5×400 will have 2 zeros. Is she correct? Explain.

_____

_____

_____

Using Mental Math to Multiply

Use compatible numbers to find each product.

1. 34 × 4 = _____ **2.** 53 × 7 = _____ **3.** 41 × 6 = _____

4. 76 × 5 = _____ **5.** 83 × 3 = _____ **6.** 28 × 8 = _____

7. 94 × 2 = _____ **8.** 16 × 4 = _____ **9.** 46 × 5 = _____

Use breaking apart to find each product.

10. 15 × 6 = _____ **11.** 95 × 4 = _____ **12.** 29 × 6 = _____

13. 83 × 7 = _____ **14.** 36 × 2 = _____ **15.** 79 × 4 = _____

16. 42 × 8 = _____ **17.** 17 × 5 = _____ **18.** 86 × 9 = _____

19. Reasonableness Quinn used breaking apart to find the product
of 37 × 4. Her answer was 124. What did she do incorrectly?

_____

_____

_____

20. Davidson's Bakery uses 9 dozen eggs to make cookies each
day. How many eggs do they use?

A 90 **B** 98 **C** 108 **D** 112

21. Writing to Explain Find the product of 53 × 6. Explain how
you found the product.

_____

_____

_____

Using Rounding to Estimate

Estimate each product.

1. 38 × 2 _____

2. 7 × 47 _____

3. 54 × 6 _____

4. 121 × 2 _____

5. 548 × 8 _____

6. 823 × 3 _____

7. 7 × 289 _____

8. 183 × 4 _____

9. 2 × 87 _____

10. 673 × 8 _____

The distance between San Francisco, California, and
Salt Lake City, Utah, is 752 miles.

11. About how many miles would a car
drive if it made 4 one-way trips?

12. About how many miles would a car
drive if it made 9 one-way trips?

_____

13. Vera has 8 boxes of paper clips. Each box has 275 paper
clips. About how many paper clips does Vera have?

A 240   **B** 1,600   **C** 2,400   **D** 24,000

14. **Writing to Explain** A large 7-story office building has
116 windows on each floor. About how many windows does
the building have in all?

_____

_____

_____

Problem Solving:
Reasonableness

For **1** and **2**, use reasonableness to decide if each answer is correct. Explain why the answer is reasonable or not. If the answer is incorrect, give the correct answer.

1. Johan is selling baseball cards for 10¢ each. He is selling 8 cards and says he'll make $8.

   _____

   _____

2. Erika is bringing cupcakes to her class. Her class sits in 4 rows of 7, so Erika estimates she'll need 35 cupcakes.

   _____

   _____

Julia is planting sunflowers. Use the table to the right to solve **3** through **5**.

3. How large will the sunflower be after the 5th week?

   _____

Weeks	Height in inches
1	16
2	32
3	48
4	64
5	

4. Viktor divided 63 by 7 and said his answer is 10. Which statement below shows why his answer is **NOT** reasonable?

   A Viktor subtracted   **C** Viktor estimated, he didn't solve

   B Viktor answered the wrong question   **D** Viktor is correct

5. **Writing to Explain** The world's largest sunflower was about 300 inches tall. Julia says her sunflower will be that tall in 10 weeks because after 2 weeks her sunflower was 32 inches and 32 × 10 = 320. Is Julia correct? If not, what did she do wrong?

   _____

   _____

Using an Expanded Algorithm

Use the array to find the partial products. Add the partial products to find the product.

1. 42
    × 8

2. 39
    × 7

3. 21
    × 4

4. 37
    × 4

5. 7 × 14 = _____

6. 3 × 52 = _____

7. 4 × 42 = _____

8. 5 × 26 = _____

9. 6 × 62 = _____

10. 9 × 76 = _____

11. Alex can type 72 words per minute. How many words can Alex type in 5 minutes? _____

12. Find 8 × 44.

   A 282   **B** 312   **C** 352   **D** 372

13. Writing to Explain Explain how you can use an array to find partial products for 4 × 36.

_____

_____

_____

Multiplying 2-Digit by 1-Digit Numbers

Find each product. Decide if your answer is reasonable.

1. $\begin{array}{r} 1\,9 \\ \times\;\; 4 \\ \hline 7\;\boxed{} \end{array}$

2. $\begin{array}{r} 2\,3 \\ \times\;\; 7 \\ \hline \boxed{}\,6\,\boxed{} \end{array}$

3. $\begin{array}{r} 5\,1 \\ \times\;\; 6 \\ \hline \boxed{}\,0\,\boxed{} \end{array}$

4. $\begin{array}{r} 39 \\ \times\;\; 7 \\ \hline \end{array}$

5. $\begin{array}{r} 48 \\ \times\;\; 5 \\ \hline \end{array}$

6. $\begin{array}{r} 53 \\ \times\;\; 7 \\ \hline \end{array}$

7. $\begin{array}{r} 29 \\ \times\;\; 8 \\ \hline \end{array}$

8. $42 \times 6 =$ _____

9. $89 \times 8 =$ _____

10. $77 \times 9 =$ _____

11. $94 \times 4 =$ _____

12. **Number Sense** Penny says that $4 \times 65 = 260$. Estimate to check Penny's answer. Is she right? Explain.

_____

_____

13. A large dump truck uses about 18 gallons of fuel in 1 hour of work. How many gallons of fuel are needed if the truck works for 5 hours? _____

14. Which of the following is a reasonable estimate for 6×82?

    A 48   **B** 480   **C** 540   **D** 550

15. **Writing to Explain** Tyrone has 6 times as many marbles as his sister Pam. Pam has 34 marbles. Louis has 202 marbles. Who has more marbles, Tyrone or Louis? Explain how you found your answer.

_____

_____

Multiplying 3-Digit by 1-Digit Numbers

Find each product. Estimate for reasonableness.

1.   352
  ×   3
  _____

2.   385
  ×   4
  _____

3.   482
  ×   8
  _____

4.   632
  ×   5
  _____

5.   219
  ×   6
  _____

6.   768
  ×   7
  _____

7.   521
  ×   4
  _____

8.   848
  ×   9
  _____

9. $7 \times 211 =$ _____

10. $6 \times 517 =$ _____

If the baseball players in the table score the same number of runs each season, how many runs will

Runs Scored in 2001

Player	Runs Scored
A	128
B	113
C	142

11. Player A score in 5 seasons?

   _____

12. Player C score in 8 seasons?

   _____

13. How many bottles of water would Tim sell if he sold 212 bottles each week for 4 weeks?

   A 800   **B** 840   **C** 848   **D** 884

14. **Writing to Explain** If you know that $8 \times 300 = 2,400$, how can you find 8×320? Explain.

   _____

   _____

   _____

Problem Solving: Draw a Picture and Write an Equation

Draw a picture to show the main idea. Then choose an operation and solve the problem.

1. A sack of potatoes weighs 20 lb and holds 200 potatoes. A sack of apples weighs 20 lb and holds 325 apples. How many more apples are there in a 20 lb sack?

   _____

2. Shawna has 35 football cards and 5 times as many baseball cards in her sports-card collection. How many baseball cards does she have?

   _____

3. A picture frame costs $8. How much will 4 frames cost?

   _____

4. The first modern electronic computer, called ENIAC, was introduced in 1946. Personal home computers were not available until 28 years later. In what year were personal home computers introduced?

   _____

Variables and Expressions

Copy and complete the table.

	k	k × 7
1.	5	5 × 7 = ▯
2.	9	9 × 7 = ▯
3.	11	▯ × 7 = 77
4.	13	▯ × 7 = 91

Complete the table for each problem.

5.

x	60	72	42	36
x ÷ 6	10	12	7	

6.

b	14	18	23	27
b + 9		27	32	36

7.

z	5	8	10	12
z × 8	40		80	96

8.

y	57	44	31	26
y − 4	53	40		22

9. When c = 4, what is the value of the expression 72 ÷ c?

A 18   **B** 20   **C** 24   **D** 28

10. Writing to Explain Explain how you could show five less than a number using an expression.

_____

_____

_____

Addition and Subtraction Expressions

Find a rule and write the missing number for each table.

1.

r	19	24	32	37
	7	12	20	

2.

a	6	9	12	15
		40		46	49

3.

s	10	15	25	30
	5	10		25

4.

b		16	19	22	26
			35	38	42

5.

w	3	6	9	12
	6		12	15

6.

n	51	42	33	24
	40	31		13

7. Evaluate the expression $15 - n$ when $n = 9$. _____

8. Which expression stands for "32 more than a number *d*"?

   A $32 \times d$ **B** $32 - d$ **C** $32 + d$ **D** $32 \div d$

9. Writing to Explain Explain how you know to use a variable in an addition or subtraction expression.

_____

_____

_____

Multiplication and Division Expressions

Find a rule and write the missing number for each table.

1.

m	6	7	8	9
	54	63		81

2.

k	14	21	49	77
		2	3	11

3.

z	54	48	39	30
	18		13	10

4.

q	2	3	4	5
	38	57	76	

5.

e	5	7	9	11
		42	54	66

6.

l	96	72	48	36
	8	6	4	

7. Evaluate the expression $48 \div n$ when $n = 6$. _____

8. Which expression means "3 times a number h"?

A $3 \times h$ **B** $3 - h$ **C** $3 + h$ **D** $3 \div h$

9. Writing to Explain How could you show the inverse operation of Exercise 5 above?

_____

_____

_____

Problem Solving:
Use Objects and Reasoning

1. Use the numbers 5 through 9 to fill the spaces in the square. Each row and column must have a sum of 15.

		1	
3			
4		2	

2. An, Larissa, Sue, and Jen are sitting in a line in a roller coaster. Larissa is sitting right in front of An. Sue is sitting right behind Jen. Jen is not sitting in the front seat. In what order are the girls sitting?

_____

3. What number am I? _____

   • My tens digit is 3 more than my thousands digit.

   • My ones digit is 2 times my hundreds digit.

   • My tens digit is 4 times my hundreds digit.

   • My tens digit is 1 more than 7.

4. Jay made a bracelet in art class using beads. He used the four beads on the right. Use the clues to guess what the pattern was.

   • The square bead is next to the triangle.

   • The hexagon is not next to the pentagon.

   • No two beads with an even number of sides are next to each other.

   • The last bead is the pentagon.

   _____

5. Mark is making a tile design to cover a rectangle. So far, he has used 2 squares and 2 triangles. How many and what shape tiles could Mark use to finish his design?

   _____

6. Draw a picture of Mark's design.

Using Mental Math to Multiply 2-Digit Numbers

Multiply. Use mental math.

1. $4 \times 30 =$ _____

2. $5 \times 90 =$ _____

3. $9 \times 200 =$ _____

4. $6 \times 500 =$ _____

5. $3 \times 600 =$ _____

6. $0 \times 600 =$ _____

7. $90 \times 70 =$ _____

8. $70 \times 400 =$ _____

9. $50 \times 800 =$ _____

10. $30 \times 800 =$ _____

11. $90 \times 500 =$ _____

12. $30 \times 4,000 =$ _____

13. **Number Sense** How many zeros are in the product of 60×900? Explain how you know.

_____

_____

Truck A can haul 400 pounds in one trip. Truck B can haul 300 pounds in one trip.

14. How many pounds can Truck A haul in 9 trips? _____

15. How many pounds can Truck B haul in 50 trips? _____

16. How many pounds can Truck A haul in 70 trips?

A 280   B 2,800   C 28,000   D 280,000

17. **Writing to Explain** There are 9 players on each basketball team in a league. Explain how you can find the total number of players in the league if there are 30 teams.

_____

_____

Estimating Products

Use rounding to estimate each product.

1. 38×29 _____

2. 71×47 _____

3. 54×76 _____

4. 121×62 _____

5. 548×28 _____

6. 823×83 _____

7. 67×289 _____

8. 183×34 _____

Use compatible numbers to estimate each product.

9. 28×87

10. 673×85

_____

_____

11. 54×347 _____

12. 65×724 _____

13. 81×643 _____

14. 44×444 _____

15. 72×285 _____

16. 61×761 _____

17. Vera has 8 boxes of paper clips. Each box has 275 paper clips. About how many paper clips does Vera have?

A 240   **B** 1,600   **C** 2,400   **D** 24,000

18. Writing to Explain A wind farm generates 330 kilowatts of electricity each day. About how many kilowatts does the wind farm produce in a week? Explain.

_____

_____

_____

Arrays and an Expanded Algorithm

Use the grid to help you complete the calculation.

1.

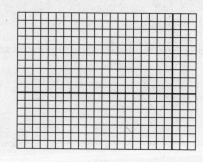

$$\begin{array}{r} 2\,3 \\ \times\ 1\,7 \end{array}$$

2.

$$\begin{array}{r} 3\,1 \\ \times\ 1\,9 \end{array}$$

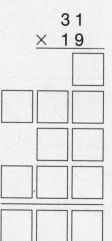

3.

$$\begin{array}{r} 2\,6 \\ \times\ 2\,2 \end{array}$$

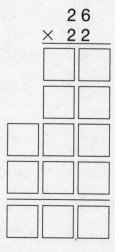

4.

$$\begin{array}{r} 3\,3 \\ \times\ 1\,4 \end{array}$$

5. $24 \times 57 =$ _____

6. $44 \times 48 =$ _____

7. A red kangaroo can cover 40 feet in 1 jump. How many feet can the red kangaroo cover in 12 jumps? _____

8. Barb exercises for 14 hours in 1 week. How many hours does she exercise in 32 weeks?

A 496 h   **B** 448 h   **C** 420 h   **D** 324 h

9. Writing to Explain Explain how the product of 16×34 is like the product of 6×34 plus 10×34.

_____

Multiplying 2-Digit Numbers by Multiples of Ten

Use the grid to show the partial products. Multiply to find the product.

1. 23 × 50

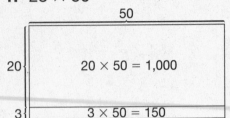

50

20 | 20 × 50 = 1,000

3 | 3 × 50 = 150

2. 30 × 82

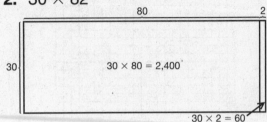

80   2

30 | 30 × 80 = 2,400

30 × 2 = 60

3. 14 × 40

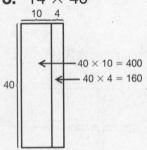

10 4

40 × 10 = 400

40 × 4 = 160

40

4. 20 × 63

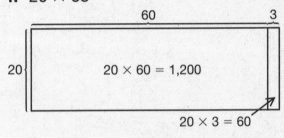

60   3

20 | 20 × 60 = 1,200

20 × 3 = 60

Use compatible numbers to estimate each product.

5. Martika works as a legal secretary. She earns $20 an hour. How much does Martika earn if she works 32 hours? _____

6. Which numbers are the partial products of 77 × 30?

  A 210 and 700   **B** 2,100 and 210   **C** 511 and 2,100   **D** 4,900 and 210

7. Writing to Explain Explain how you can find the product of 40 × 16 by breaking apart the numbers.

_____

_____

_____

Multiplying 2-Digit by 2-Digit Numbers

1.
```
   54
×  17
```

2.
```
   36
×  20
```

3.
```
   53
×  12
```

4.
```
   48
×  46
```

5.
```
   37
×  83
```

6.
```
   62
×  17
```

7.
```
   91
×  49
```

8.
```
   28
×  56
```

9.
```
   70
×  39
```

10.
```
   58
×  90
```

11.
```
   97
×  42
```

12.
```
   64
×  88
```

13. A carton holds 24 bottles of juice. How many juice bottles are in 15 cartons?

_____

14. How much do 21 bushels of sweet corn weigh?

_____

Vegetable	Weight of 1 Bushel
Asparagus	24 lb
Beets	52 lb
Carrots	50 lb
Sweet corn	35 lb

15. How much do 18 bushels of asparagus weigh?

_____

16. How much more do 13 bushels of beets weigh than 13 bushels of carrots?   _____

17. Which of the following is a reasonable answer for 92 × 98?

   A 1,800   **B** 9,000   **C** 10,000   **D** 90,000

18. **Writing to Explain** Garth is multiplying 29 × 16. He has 174 after multiplying the ones and 290 after multiplying the tens. Explain how Garth can find the final product.

_____

Special Cases

1. $\begin{array}{r} 200 \\ \times\ 30 \\ \hline \end{array}$
2. $\begin{array}{r} 200 \\ \times\ 20 \\ \hline \end{array}$
3. $\begin{array}{r} 300 \\ \times\ 25 \\ \hline \end{array}$
4. $\begin{array}{r} 400 \\ \times\ 80 \\ \hline \end{array}$

5. $\begin{array}{r} 325 \\ \times\ 30 \\ \hline \end{array}$
6. $\begin{array}{r} 800 \\ \times\ 70 \\ \hline \end{array}$
7. $\begin{array}{r} 500 \\ \times\ 70 \\ \hline \end{array}$
8. $\begin{array}{r} 800 \\ \times\ 50 \\ \hline \end{array}$

9. $\begin{array}{r} 800 \\ \times\ 15 \\ \hline \end{array}$
10. $\begin{array}{r} 300 \\ \times\ 50 \\ \hline \end{array}$
11. $\begin{array}{r} 600 \\ \times\ 50 \\ \hline \end{array}$
12. $\begin{array}{r} 100 \\ \times\ 60 \\ \hline \end{array}$

13. **Number Sense** Would the answer to 20×500 have three zeroes or 4? Explain.

    _____

    _____

Use the table at right for problems **14** and **15**.

14. How many pencils are in 30 boxes?

Supplies	Per Box
Pencils	150
Pens	190

    _____

15. How many pens are in 200 boxes?

    _____

16. Hailey sold 120 bottles of water in 1 week. How many bottles could she sell in 20 weeks?

    A 240 **B** 1,220 **C** 2,400 **D** 24,000

17. **Writing to Explain** How could you use the product
    $10 \times 42 = 420$ to find the product of 5×42?

    _____

    _____

Problem Solving:
Two-Question Problems

For **1** and **2**, use the answer from the first problem to solve the second problem.

1. **Problem 1:** Francisco reads 75 pages every week for a summer reading program. If there are about 4 weeks in a month, then how many pages can Francisco read in a month?

_____

Problem 2: How many pages will Francisco read in the three months of summer?

_____

2. **Problem 1:** Mr. Dunn drives a 15-mile round trip every day to work. If Mr. Dunn works five days a week how many miles does he drive?

_____

Problem 2: Mr. Dunn estimates he uses 3 gallons of gas over the course of a week. How many miles per gallon does his car get?

_____

3. A company buys printer paper in a box which contains 8 packages. If each package of paper costs 3 dollars, how much does a box of paper cost? Which number sentence shows how much 12 boxes will cost?

   A $8 + 3 \times 12$ **B** $24 \div 12$ **C** $24 + 12$ **D** 24×12

4. **Writing to Explain** There are 12 plots in a community garden. What information would you need to know if you wanted to know how much area can be farmed in the community garden? Explain.

_____

_____

_____

Using Mental Math to Divide

Divide. Use mental math.

1. $250 \div 5 =$ _____

2. $1,400 \div 2 =$ _____

3. $300 \div 5 =$ _____

4. $1,600 \div 4 =$ _____

5. $240 \div 8 =$ _____

6. $36,000 \div 4 =$ _____

7. $16,000 \div 2 =$ _____

8. $270 \div 3 =$ _____

9. $4,200 \div 7 =$ _____

10. $640 \div 8 =$ _____

11. $2,000 \div 5 =$ _____

12. $320 \div 8 =$ _____

13. $12,000 \div 2 =$ _____

14. $1,600 \div 8 =$ _____

The fourth grade performed a play based on the story of Cinderella. There was one chair for each person present.

15. On Friday, 140 people came to the play. The chairs in the auditorium were arranged in 7 equal rows. How many chairs were in each row? _____

16. There were 8 equal rows set up for Saturday's performance. There were 240 people at the play on Saturday. How many chairs were in each row? _____

17. Which is the quotient of $56,000 \div 8$?

    A 400   **B** 4,000   **C** 700   **D** 7,000

18. **Writing to Explain** Explain why the following answer is not correct: $1,000 \div 5 = \underline{2,000}$.

_____

_____

_____

Estimating Quotients

Estimate each quotient.

1. 82 ÷ 4 _____

2. 580 ÷ 3 _____

3. 96 ÷ 5 _____

4. 811 ÷ 2 _____

5. 194 ÷ 6 _____

6. 207 ÷ 7 _____

7. 282 ÷ 4 _____

8. 479 ÷ 8 _____

9. Jacqui is writing a book. If she needs to
write 87 pages in 9 days, about how
many pages will she write each day? _____

10. Wade wants to give 412 of his marbles to
10 of his friends. If he gives each friend
the same number of marbles, about
how many will each friend receive? _____

11. Which is the best estimate for 502 ÷ 6?

   A 60   **B** 70   **C** 80   **D** 90

12. **Writing to Explain** You are using division to determine
how much whole wheat flour to use in a bread recipe. Is an
estimated answer good enough?

   _____

   _____

Dividing with Remainders

Divide. You may use counters or pictures to help.

1. $4\overline{)27}$ 2. $6\overline{)32}$ 3. $7\overline{)17}$ 4. $9\overline{)29}$

5. $8\overline{)27}$ 6. $3\overline{)27}$ 7. $5\overline{)28}$ 8. $4\overline{)35}$

9. $2\overline{)19}$ 10. $7\overline{)30}$ 11. $3\overline{)17}$ 12. $9\overline{)16}$

If you arrange these items into equal rows, tell how many will be in each row and how many will be left over.

13. 26 shells into 3 rows   _____

14. 19 pennies into 5 rows   _____

15. 17 balloons into 7 rows   _____

16. **Reasonableness** Ms. Nikkel wants to divide her class of 23 students into 4 equal teams. Is this reasonable? Why or why not?

_____

_____

17. Which is the remainder for the quotient of $79 \div 8$?

A 7   **B** 6   **C** 5   **D** 4

18. **Writing to Explain** Pencils are sold in packages of 5. Explain why you need 6 packages in order to have enough for 27 students.

_____

_____

Connecting Models and Symbols

Draw pictures to tell how many are in each group and how many are left over.

1. 57 CDs in 8 organizers

2. 62 stickers on 5 rolls

_____

_____

3. 44 plants in 6 rows

4. 37 chairs for 9 tables

_____

_____

In **5** through **8**, use the model to complete each division sentence.

5. 27 ÷ ☐ = ☐ R3

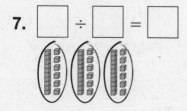

6. ☐ ÷ 11 = ☐

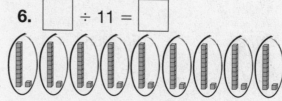

7. ☐ ÷ ☐ = ☐

8. ☐ ÷ ☐ = ☐ R ☐

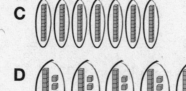

9. Ken has 72 marbles. He decides to share them with his friends so they can play a game. Which of the following models shows Ken sharing his marbles?

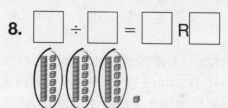

10. Writing to Explain At Mr. Horne's farm there are 53 cows. There are 4 people who milk the cows each day. Does each person milk the same number of cows? Use a model to help you.

_____

_____

Dividing 2-Digit by 1-Digit Numbers

1.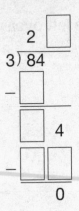

2.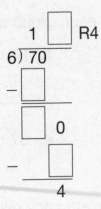

3.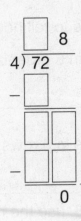

4. 2)72

5. 5)86

6. 7)94

7. 3)39

8. 8)99

9. 5)87

10. 2)96

11. 3)43

Mrs. Thomas is planning to provide snacks for 96 fourth graders when they go on a field trip to the aquarium. Each student will receive 1 of each snack. Using the bar to the right, how many packages of each snack does Mrs. Thomas need?

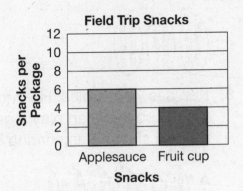

12. fruit cups _____

13. applesauce _____

14. Which is the remainder of 27 ÷ 4?

A 1   **B** 2   **C** 3   **D** 4

15. Writing to Explain Explain how to find the number of leftover pencils if Wendy wants to share 37 pencils with 9 people.

_____

_____

_____

Dividing 3-Digit by 1-Digit Numbers

In **1** through **8**, use place-value blocks to help you divide.

1. $4\overline{)412}$ 2. $6\overline{)936}$ 3. $7\overline{)798}$ 4. $7\overline{)806}$

5. $3\overline{)420}$ 6. $5\overline{)619}$ 7. $7\overline{)842}$ 8. $8\overline{)856}$

9. A train can hold 136 people in rows of 4 seats each. How many 4-seat rows are there? _____

10. A song has 540 beats. If the song is 3 minutes long, how many beats per minute does the song have? _____

11. **Geometry** A pizza has 360 degrees. If the pizza is divided into 8 equal slices, how many degrees does each slice measure? _____

12. Harvey has 516 stamps in his collection. He has 6 stamp books. How many stamps are in each book? _____

13. Zeeshan has collected 812 autographs. Each autograph is either from a baseball star, a football star, a movie star, or a rock star. He has an equal number of autographs for each group. How many autographs does he have in each group? _____

14. Nicole has 189 tea bags. There are 4 different flavors of tea. What information do you need to find how many tea bags Nicole has of each flavor?

    A The number of flavors

    B The number of tea bags

    C If a tea bag can be divided into fourths

    D If there are an equal number of tea bags for each flavor

15. An ant has 6 legs. There are 870 legs in José's ant farm. How many ants are there in his ant farm?

    A 14 R5 **B** 145 **C** 864 **D** 5,220

16. **Writing to Explain** Jeff has 171 DVDs. He has 3 shelves that can each hold 55 DVDs. Does he need to buy another shelf?

_____

Deciding Where to Start Dividing

Complete each calculation.

1.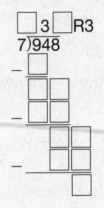

2.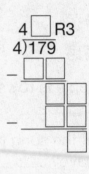

3.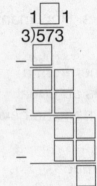

4.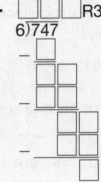

5. 2)587

6. 8)747

7. 9)411

8. 7)698

9. Gerald distributes 582 brochures to 3 businesses each week. How many brochures does each business get?

A 159   **B** 174   **C** 194   **D** 264

10. Writing to Explain Write and solve a word problem for 456 ÷ 6.

_____

_____

_____

Factors

For **1** through **12**, find all the factors of each number.

1. 54

2. 17

3. 28

4. 31

_____

_____

5. 44

6. 47

7. 77

8. 71

_____

_____

9. 65

10. 23

11. 57

12. 24

_____

_____

13. Karl's mother buys 60 party favors to give out as gifts during Karl's birthday party. Which number of guests will NOT let her divide the party favors evenly among the guests?

A 12

B 15

C 20

D 25

14. Writing to Explain Mrs. Fisher has 91 watches on display at her store. She says she can arrange them into rows and columns without any watches left over. Mr. Fisher says that she can only make 1 row with all 91 watches. Who is right and why?

_____

_____

_____

Prime and Composite Numbers

In **1** through **16**, write whether each number is prime or composite.

1. 81 _____

2. 43 _____

3. 572 _____

4. 63 _____

5. 53 _____

6. 87 _____

7. 3 _____

8. 27 _____

9. 88 _____

10. 19 _____

11. 69 _____

12. 79 _____

13. 3,235 _____

14. 1,212 _____

15. 57 _____

16. 17 _____

17. Mr. Gerry's class has 19 students, Ms. Vernon's class has 21 students, and Mr. Singh's class has 23 students. Whose class has a composite number of students?

_____

18. Every prime number larger than 10 has a digit in the ones place that is included in which set of numbers below?

A 1, 3, 7, 9

C 0, 2, 4, 5, 6, 8

B 1, 3, 5, 9

D 1, 3, 7

19. Writing to Explain Marla says that every number in the nineties is composite. Jackie says that one number in the nineties is prime. Who is correct? Explain your answer.

_____

_____

_____

Problem Solving:
Multiple-Step Problems

Write and answer the hidden question or questions.
Then solve the problem. Write your answer in a
complete sentence.

County Fair Admission	
Adults	$5.00
Students	$3.00
Children	$2.00

1. Mario and his family went to the county
   fair. They bought 2 adult passes and
   3 children's passes. What was the
   total cost for the family?

   _____

   _____

   _____

2. A bus has 12 rows with 1 seat in each row on one side and
   12 rows with 2 seats in each row on the other side. How
   many seats does the bus have altogether?

   _____

   _____

   _____

3. **Writing to Explain** Write a problem about going to the laundromat
   that has a hidden question. A single load of laundry costs $2 and a
   double load costs $4. Solve your problem.

   _____

   _____

Points, Lines, and Planes

Use geometric terms to describe what is shown. Be as specific as possible.

1.

_____

2.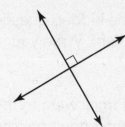

3.

X

_____

4.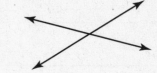

_____

5. Name two lines.

_____

6. Name two lines that are perpendicular.

_____

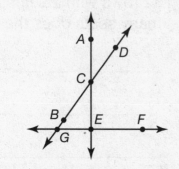

7. Which two lines are parallel?

A $\overleftrightarrow{HK}$ and $\overleftrightarrow{JL}$ C $\overleftrightarrow{HJ}$ and $\overleftrightarrow{JK}$

B $\overleftrightarrow{HJ}$ and $\overleftrightarrow{JL}$ D $\overleftrightarrow{HJ}$ and $\overleftrightarrow{LM}$

8. **Writing to Explain** Describe a point.

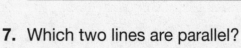
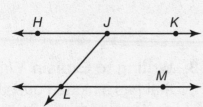
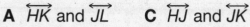

_____

_____

Lines, Rays, and Angles

Use geometric terms to describe what is shown. Be as specific as possible.

1.

_____

2.

_____

3.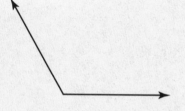

_____

4.

_____

5. Name two line segments.

_____

6. Name two obtuse angles.

_____

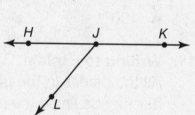

7. Which is the geometric term for ∠HJK?

   A Acute angle   **C** Right angle

   B Obtuse angle   **D** Straight angle

8. **Writing to Explain** Describe an acute angle.

_____

_____

Name _____

Measuring Angles

For Exercises **1** through **4**, measure the angle.

1. _____ **2.** _____ **3.** _____ **4.** _____

For Exercises **5** through **8**, draw the angle:

5. 45°   **6.** 145°   **7.** 60°   **8.** 180°

9. Rich has 3 pieces of pizza. Each pizza end forms a 20° angle.
   If all of the pieces were placed together what would the size
   of the angle be?

   _____

10. Stuart, Sam, Sue, and Sally have equal-sized pieces of pie.
    When the 4 pieces are put together they form a 100° angle.
    What is the angle of each piece?

    A 100°   **B** 50°   **C** 25°   **D** 15°

11. **Writing to Explain** Gail and her 3 friends all share half a pie.
    All the pieces in the pie put together make up 180°. Gail and
    her friends finish the pie and they each eat an equal piece.
    They believe each piece has an angle equal to 25°. Are their
    calculations correct? Explain.

    _____

    _____

    _____

Polygons

Draw an example of each polygon. How many sides and vertices does each one have?

1. Quadrilateral

2. Octagon

3. Hexagon

The map shows the shapes of buildings in Polygon Park. Identify the polygons that are lettered.

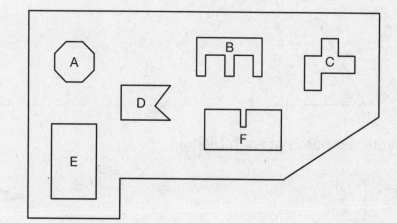

4. A

_____

5. D

_____

6. C

_____

7. B

_____

8. E

_____

9. F

_____

10. Which is the point where sides meet in a polygon?

A edge　　　　**B** endpoint　　　　**C** side　　　　**D** vertex

11. Writing to Explain Describe two polygons by the number of vertices and sides each has.

_____

Triangles

Classify each triangle by its sides and then by its angles.

1. 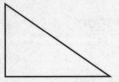 _____

2. 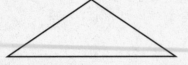 _____

3. _____

Write the name of each triangle.

4.

5.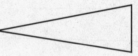

_____   _____

6. Which is a triangle with one right angle?

   A Equilateral triangle **B** Obtuse triangle **C** Right triangle **D** Acute triangle

7. **Writing to Explain** Why can't a triangle have more than one obtuse angle?

_____

_____

_____

Quadrilaterals

Write all the names you can use for each quadrilateral.

1.

_____

2.

_____

3.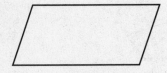

_____

4.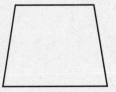

5.

_____   _____

6. Which is **NOT** a quadrilateral?

   A rhombus   **B** rectangle   **C** right triangle   **D** trapezoid

7. **Writing to Explain** Explain why a square can never be a trapezoid.

_____

_____

_____

Problem Solving:
Make and Test Generalizations

For Exercises **1** through **3**, use the images to make a generalization and test your answer.

1.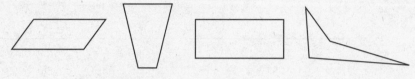

_____

2.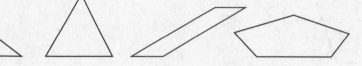

_____

3.

_____

_____

4. Which statement below is a good generalization about all rectangular prisms?

  A All rectangular prisms have same-sized faces.

  B All rectangular prisms have 12 edges.

  C All rectangular prisms are cubes.

  D All rectangular prisms have 1 net.

5. **Writing to Explain** Try to draw a triangle with 2 right or obtuse angles. What generalizations can you make about the angles of a triangle? Explain.

_____

_____

Regions and Sets

Write a fraction for the part of the region below that is shaded.

1.

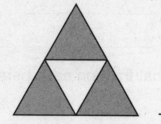 _____

2.

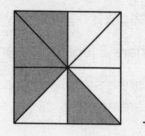 _____

Shade in the models to show each fraction.

3. $\frac{2}{4}$ ◯ ◯
◯ ◯

4. $\frac{7}{10}$ ☐ ☐ ☐ ☐ ☐
☐ ☐ ☐ ☐ ☐

5. What fraction of the pizza is cheese?

_____

6. What fraction of the pizza is mushroom?

_____

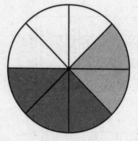

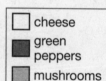
☐ cheese
■ green peppers
▨ mushrooms

7. Number Sense Is $\frac{1}{4}$ of 12 greater than $\frac{1}{4}$ of 8? Explain your answer.

_____

_____

8. A set has 12 squares. Which is the number of squares in $\frac{1}{3}$ of the set?

A 3   **B** 4   **C** 6   **D** 9

9. Writing to Explain Explain why $\frac{1}{2}$ of Region A is not larger than $\frac{1}{2}$ of Region B.

_____

_____

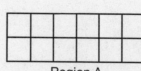

Region A   Region B

Fractions and Division

What fraction does each person get when they share equally?

1. Eight friends share 3 bags of toys. _____

2. Five people share 2 jugs of water. _____

Five friends are sharing supplies on a camping trip. Tell what fraction each person gets when they share equally.

3. Two boxes of trail mix. _____

4. Three packages of water purifying tablets. _____

5. **Reasoning** Four people each bought 2 bottles of Vermont maple syrup. Each person plans to share their bottles with 3 friends. How much does each person get? _____

6. Which model represents 6 people sharing 1 five-foot sub?

A

C

B

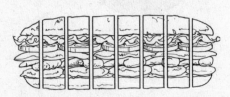

D

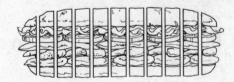

7. **Writing to Explain** Several friends are taking turns flying a kite. Each friend flies the kite for the same amount of time. They spend 6 hours flying the kite altogether. Explain what information you need to find how long each friend flew the kite.

_____

_____

Estimating Fractional Amounts

Estimate the fractional amount of each that is shaded.

1.

2.

3.

_____   _____   _____

4. **Reasonableness** Is $\frac{1}{6}$ a reasonable estimate for the shaded part in the region to the right? Explain.

_____

_____

Estimate the fraction that should be written at each point.

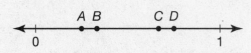

5. A _____   6. B _____   7. C _____   8. D _____

9. Part of the region to the right is shaded. Which is the best estimate?

A $\frac{3}{3}$ B $\frac{2}{3}$ C $\frac{1}{3}$ D $\frac{0}{3}$

10. **Writing to Explain** Explain how you estimated the shaded region in Exercise 9.

_____

_____

_____

_____

_____

Name _____

Equivalent Fractions

Find the missing number.

1. $\frac{1}{2} = \frac{\square}{12}$

2. $\frac{6}{10} = \frac{\square}{5}$

3. $\frac{4}{16} = \frac{\square}{4}$

4. $2\frac{4}{20} = 2\frac{\square}{40}$

_____   _____   _____   _____

Multiply or divide to find an equivalent fraction.

5. $\frac{11}{22}$

6. $\frac{6}{36}$

7. $\frac{9}{10}$

8. $\frac{5}{35}$

9. $\frac{7}{12}$

_____   _____   _____   _____   _____

10. Is $\frac{2}{14}$ equivalent to $\frac{3}{7}$? _____

11. In Mark's collection of antique bottles, $\frac{4}{9}$ of the bottles are dark green.
    Write three equivalent fractions for $\frac{4}{9}$.

    _____

12. Write a pair of equivalent fractions for the picture above.

    _____

13. At the air show, $\frac{1}{3}$ of the airplanes were gliders. Which fraction is not an
    equivalent fraction for $\frac{1}{3}$?

    A $\frac{5}{15}$ B $\frac{7}{21}$ C $\frac{6}{24}$ D $\frac{9}{27}$

14. **Writing to Explain** In Missy's sports-cards collection, $\frac{5}{7}$ of the cards are
    baseball. In Frank's collection, $\frac{12}{36}$ are baseball. Frank says they have the
    same fraction of baseball cards. Is he correct?

    _____

    _____

Fractions in Simplest Form

For **1** through **18**, write each fraction in simplest form. If it is in simplest form, write "simplest form."

1. $\frac{13}{14}$ _____

2. $\frac{7}{8}$ _____

3. $\frac{1}{23}$ _____

4. $\frac{15}{20}$ _____

5. $\frac{2}{18}$ _____

6. $\frac{6}{30}$ _____

7. $\frac{5}{18}$ _____

8. $\frac{13}{26}$ _____

9. $\frac{9}{12}$ _____

10. $\frac{7}{21}$ _____

11. $\frac{7}{10}$ _____

12. $\frac{40}{50}$ _____

13. $\frac{18}{36}$ _____

14. $\frac{25}{35}$ _____

15. $\frac{12}{14}$ _____

16. $\frac{8}{9}$ _____

17. $\frac{60}{80}$ _____

18. $\frac{2}{8}$ _____

19. Sheldon has scored $\frac{6}{18}$ of the points in a basketball game. How can you use division to simplify the fraction of the points he scored? What is $\frac{6}{18}$ in simplest form?

_____

_____

_____

20. What is the simplest form of the fraction $\frac{40}{80}$?

A $\frac{1}{4}$ **B** $\frac{4}{8}$ **C** $\frac{2}{4}$ **D** $\frac{1}{2}$

21. **Writing to Explain** If the numerator of a fraction is a prime number, can the fraction be simplified? Why or why not?

_____

_____

Improper Fractions and Mixed Numbers

Write each mixed number as an improper fraction.

1. $3\frac{2}{5}$ _____

2. $6\frac{1}{4}$ _____

3. $2\frac{1}{12}$ _____

4. $2\frac{7}{9}$ _____

Write each improper fraction as a mixed number or whole number.

5. $\frac{12}{5}$ _____

6. $\frac{27}{9}$ _____

7. $\frac{32}{3}$ _____

8. $\frac{20}{12}$ _____

9. **Number Sense** Matt had to write $3\frac{8}{24}$ as an improper fraction. Write how you would tell Matt the easiest way to do so.

_____

_____

_____

_____

10. Jill has $\frac{11}{8}$ ounces of trail mix. Write the weight of Jill's trail mix as a mixed number.   _____

11. Nick had $1\frac{3}{4}$ gal of milk. Write the amount of milk Nick has as an improper fraction.   _____

12. Which is **NOT** an improper fraction equal to 8?

    A $\frac{24}{3}$ B $\frac{49}{7}$ C $\frac{56}{7}$ D $\frac{64}{8}$

13. **Writing to Explain** Write three different improper fractions that equal $4\frac{2}{3}$. (Hint: find equivalent fractions.)

_____

_____

Comparing Fractions

Write > or < for each $\bigcirc$. You may use fraction strips to help.

1. $\frac{1}{2} \bigcirc \frac{3}{13}$ 2. $\frac{8}{9} \bigcirc \frac{5}{9}$ 3. $\frac{3}{8} \bigcirc \frac{11}{22}$

4. $\frac{3}{3} \bigcirc \frac{7}{8}$ 5. $\frac{3}{5} \bigcirc \frac{1}{3}$ 6. $\frac{1}{4} \bigcirc \frac{2}{4}$

7. $\frac{5}{6} \bigcirc \frac{5}{8}$ 8. $\frac{7}{12} \bigcirc \frac{4}{5}$ 9. $\frac{3}{7} \bigcirc \frac{6}{7}$

10. **Number Sense** Explain how you know that $\frac{21}{30}$ is greater than $\frac{2}{3}$.

_____

_____

_____

11. Tina completed $\frac{2}{3}$ of her homework before dinner.
George completed $\frac{4}{7}$ of his homework before dinner.
Who completed a greater fraction of homework? _____

12. Jackson played a video game for $\frac{1}{6}$ hour. Hailey
played a video game for $\frac{1}{3}$ hour. Who played
the video game for a greater amount of time? _____

13. Which fraction is greater than $\frac{3}{4}$?

     A $\frac{5}{9}$ **B** $\frac{17}{24}$ **C** $\frac{15}{20}$ **D** $\frac{7}{9}$

14. **Writing to Explain** James says that $\frac{5}{5}$ is greater than $\frac{99}{100}$.
Is he correct? Explain.

_____

_____

_____

_____

Ordering Fractions

Order the fractions from least to greatest.

1. $\frac{1}{9}, \frac{7}{8}, \frac{5}{6}$

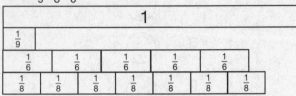

2. $\frac{1}{2}, \frac{7}{12}, \frac{4}{10}$

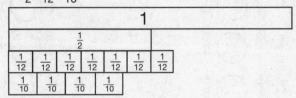

3. $\frac{3}{9}, \frac{1}{4}, \frac{5}{12}$

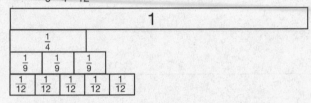

4. $\frac{4}{15}, \frac{2}{5}, \frac{1}{3}$

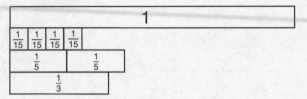

Find equivalent fractions with a common denominator and order from least to greatest.

5. $\frac{2}{3}, \frac{1}{2}, \frac{5}{12}$ _____

6. $\frac{3}{8}, \frac{1}{3}, \frac{3}{4}$ _____

7. $\frac{3}{7}, \frac{1}{9}, \frac{2}{3}$ _____

8. $\frac{7}{12}, \frac{2}{6}, \frac{7}{8}$ _____

9. $\frac{3}{42}, \frac{5}{6}, \frac{7}{21}$ _____

10. $\frac{9}{15}, \frac{1}{3}, \frac{2}{5}$ _____

11. Which fraction is greater than $\frac{2}{3}$?

A $\frac{1}{12}$ **B** $\frac{11}{36}$ **C** $\frac{5}{16}$ **D** $\frac{5}{7}$

12. **Writing to Explain** Explain how you know that $\frac{15}{30}$ is greater than $\frac{1}{3}$ but less than $\frac{2}{3}$?

_____

_____

_____

_____

Problem Solving:
Writing to Explain

1. Mary has 23 marbles. $\frac{7}{23}$ of the marbles are yellow and $\frac{13}{23}$ of the marbles are blue. The rest of the marbles are green. How many marbles are green? Explain how you know.

_____

_____

_____

_____

2. Adam wants to compare the fractions $\frac{2}{5}$, $\frac{1}{6}$, and $\frac{1}{3}$. He wants to order them from least to greatest and rewrite them so they all have the same denominator. Explain how Adam can rewrite the fractions.

_____

_____

_____

3. Adam used the three fractions to make a circle graph and colored each a different color. What fraction of the graph is not colored? Explain your answer.

_____

_____

_____

Adding and Subtracting Fractions with Like Denominators

For **1** through **15**, add or subtract the fractions and write the answer in simplest form. You may use fraction strips to help.

1. $\frac{1}{8} + \frac{3}{8} =$ _____

2. $\frac{8}{10} + \frac{1}{10} =$ _____

3. $\frac{1}{3} + \frac{1}{3} =$ _____

4. $\frac{3}{8}$
$+ \frac{3}{8}$
_____

5. $\frac{1}{9}$
$+ \frac{4}{9}$
_____

6. $\frac{3}{6}$
$+ \frac{2}{6}$
_____

7. $\frac{9}{12} - \frac{2}{12} =$ _____

8. $\frac{4}{8} - \frac{2}{8} =$ _____

9. $\frac{6}{10} - \frac{1}{10} =$ _____

10. $\frac{5}{8}$
$- \frac{2}{8}$
_____

11. $\frac{7}{10}$
$- \frac{1}{10}$
_____

12. $\frac{8}{10}$
$- \frac{4}{10}$
_____

13. $\frac{1}{6}$
$+ \frac{2}{6}$
_____

14. $\frac{1}{7}$
$+ \frac{1}{7}$
_____

15. $\frac{1}{4}$
$+ \frac{1}{4}$
_____

16. Jacob is making a stew. The stew calls for $\frac{3}{8}$ cup of rice. If he doubles the recipe, how much rice will he need? Write your answer in simplest form.

_____

17. Which of the following fractions is not an equivalent fraction to $\frac{1}{3}$?

A $\frac{3}{9}$ **B** $\frac{2}{6}$ **C** $\frac{3}{6}$ **D** $\frac{4}{12}$

18. **Writing to Explain** Gerry folded $\frac{3}{8}$ of the pile of shirts. Molly folded $\frac{1}{8}$ of the pile of shirts. Together, did they fold more than half the shirts? Explain your answer.

_____

_____

Adding Fractions with Unlike Denominators

Write the answers in simplest form.

1. $\frac{1}{6} + \frac{1}{3} =$ _____

2. $\frac{1}{5} + \frac{1}{10} =$ _____

3. $\frac{1}{4} + \frac{1}{2} =$ _____

4. $\frac{2}{3} + \frac{1}{6} =$ _____

5. $\frac{1}{4} + \frac{2}{5} =$ _____

6. $\frac{1}{4} + \frac{1}{6} =$ _____

7. $\frac{2}{5} + \frac{1}{6} =$ _____

8. $\frac{1}{4} + \frac{5}{8} =$ _____

9. $\frac{5}{12} + \frac{1}{4}$

10. $\frac{1}{5} + \frac{3}{10}$

11. $\frac{2}{5} + \frac{1}{2}$

12. $\frac{1}{12} + \frac{2}{3}$

_____   _____   _____   _____

13. A recipe calls for $\frac{1}{4}$ cup of whole wheat flour and $\frac{1}{2}$ cup of white flour. How many cups of flour are needed in all? _____

14. **Reasoning** To trim a costume, you need $\frac{1}{2}$ yard of lace at the neck and $\frac{1}{6}$ yard at the wrist. How much lace is needed? _____

15. **Algebra** If $n = \frac{9}{14}$, then $n + \frac{2}{7} =$ _____

16. For the addition $\frac{1}{6} + \frac{2}{3}$, which sum is **NOT** correct?

A $\frac{9}{12}$ **B** $\frac{5}{6}$ **C** $\frac{15}{18}$ **D** $\frac{20}{24}$

17. **Writing to Explain** What common denominator would you use to add $\frac{1}{3}$, $\frac{1}{4}$, and $\frac{1}{12}$? Explain.

_____

Subtracting Fractions with Unlike Denominators

Write the answers in simplest form.

1. $\frac{1}{2} - \frac{1}{8}$

2. $\frac{7}{8} - \frac{1}{2}$

3. $\frac{11}{15} - \frac{2}{5}$

4. $\frac{8}{9} - \frac{1}{3}$

_____

_____

_____

_____

5. $\frac{5}{6} - \frac{1}{4}$

6. $\frac{3}{4} - \frac{2}{5}$

7. $\frac{9}{16} - \frac{1}{8}$

8. $\frac{9}{10} - \frac{3}{4}$

_____

_____

_____

_____

9. $\begin{array}{r} \frac{5}{8} \\ - \frac{3}{16} \\ \hline \end{array}$

10. $\begin{array}{r} \frac{5}{12} \\ - \frac{1}{6} \\ \hline \end{array}$

11. $\begin{array}{r} \frac{3}{4} \\ - \frac{1}{6} \\ \hline \end{array}$

12. $\begin{array}{r} \frac{7}{8} \\ - \frac{1}{6} \\ \hline \end{array}$

13. There was $\frac{7}{8}$ of a pizza left at 1:00. Then Lou ate $\frac{1}{4}$ of the original pizza. How much was left then?

A $\frac{5}{8}$

B $\frac{6}{8}$

C $\frac{7}{8}$

D $\frac{3}{4}$

14. Writing to Explain In what way is subtracting fractions with unlike denominators like adding fractions with unlike denominators?

_____

_____

Problem Solving: Draw a Picture and Write an Equation

1. Jamie bought $\frac{5}{8}$ pound of wheat flour. He also bought $\frac{1}{4}$ pound of white flour. How much flour did he buy?

_____

2. Katie is $\frac{3}{5}$ of the way to Brianna's house. Larry is $\frac{7}{10}$ of the way to Brianna's house. How much closer to Brianna's house is Larry?

_____

3. Nina practiced the trumpet for $\frac{5}{9}$ hour. Santiago practiced the trumpet for $\frac{2}{3}$ hour. How much longer did Santiago practice than Nina?

_____

4. Ned caught $\frac{1}{3}$ pound of fish. Sarah caught $\frac{5}{12}$ pound of fish. Jessa caught $\frac{1}{6}$ pound of fish. Which bar diagram shows how to find how many pounds of fish they caught altogether?

A $\vdash$— ? pounds in all —$\dashv$

$\frac{2}{6}$	$\frac{2}{6}$	$\frac{1}{6}$

C $\vdash$——— ? pounds in all ———$\dashv$

$\frac{3}{12}$	$\frac{5}{12}$	$\frac{6}{12}$

B $\vdash$— ? pounds in all —$\dashv$

$\frac{1}{3}$	$\frac{5}{12}$	$\frac{1}{6}$

D $\vdash$? pounds in all$\dashv$

$\frac{1}{12}$	$\frac{5}{12}$	$\frac{1}{12}$

5. **Writing to Explain** John added the numerators of several fractions with unlike denominators. What should John have done first?

_____

_____

Decimal Place Value

Write the word form and decimal for each shaded part.

1.   _____

2.   _____

For each fact, shade a grid to show the part of the population of each country that lives in cities.

3. In Jamaica, 0.5 of the people live in cities.

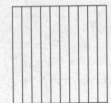

4. Only 0.11 of the population of Uganda live in cities.

5. In Norway, 0.72 of the people live in cities.

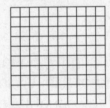

6. Which grid shows fourteen hundredths?

A   **B**   **C**   **D**

7. Writing to Explain Explain why one column in a hundredths grid is equal to one column in a tenths grid.

_____

_____

_____

Comparing and Ordering Decimals

Compare. Write $>$, $<$, or $=$ for each $\bigcirc$.

1. 0.31 $\bigcirc$ 0.41   **2.** 1.9 $\bigcirc$ 0.95   **3.** 0.09 $\bigcirc$ 0.1

4. 2.70 $\bigcirc$ 2.7   **5.** 0.81 $\bigcirc$ 0.79   **6.** 2.12 $\bigcirc$ 2.21

Order the numbers from least to greatest.

7. 0.37, 0.41, 0.31   **8.** 1.16, 1.61, 6.11

_____   _____

9. 7.9, 7.91, 7.09, 7.19   **10.** 1.45, 1.76, 1.47, 1.67

_____   _____

Margaret has three cats. Sophie weighs 4.27 lb, Tigger weighs 6.25 lb, and Ghost weighs 4.7 lb.

11. Which cat has the greatest weight?   _____

12. Which cat weighs the least?   _____

13. Which group of numbers is ordered from least to greatest?

   A 0.12, 1.51, 0.65

   B 5.71, 5.4, 0.54

   C 0.4, 0.09, 0.41

   D 0.05, 0.51, 1.5

14. **Writing to Explain** Darrin put the numbers 7.25, 7.52, 5.72, and 5.27 in order from greatest to least. Is his work correct? Explain.

_____

_____

Fractions and Decimals

Write a fraction and a decimal to show how much is shaded.

1.

_____

2.

_____

3.
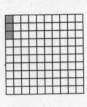

_____

Draw a model that shows each decimal.

4. 0.16

5. 1.7

6. 0.78

Write each fraction as a decimal.

7. $\frac{1}{100}$

8. $9\frac{4}{10}$

9. $\frac{6}{10}$

10. $\frac{17}{100}$

_____   _____   _____   _____

Write each decimal as a fraction in its simplest form.

11. 0.5

12. 0.70

13. 0.3

14. 3.60

_____   _____   _____   _____

15. In the decimal models, how many strips equal 10 small squares?

A 70 strips   **B** 10 strips   **C** 7 strips   **D** 1 strip

16. Writing to Explain Explain the steps you would take to write $\frac{36}{10}$ as a decimal.

_____

_____

_____

Fractions and Decimals on the Number Line

Use the number line to name the fraction or decimal that should be written at each point.

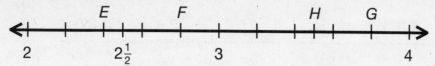

1. E _____   2. F _____   3. G _____   4. H _____

Identify the correct point on the number line for each fraction or decimal.

5. 8.3 _____   6. $7\frac{3}{5}$ _____   7. 7.7 _____   8. 8.2 _____

9. Eamon used a number line to compare two numbers, 0.48 and $\frac{3}{5}$. One number was less than $\frac{1}{2}$ and the other number was greater than $\frac{1}{2}$. Which number was less than $\frac{1}{2}$? _____

10. Which of the following choices is not correct?

    A $0.43 < \frac{4}{5}$ **B** $\frac{2}{3} > 0.07$ **C** $\frac{1}{2} > 0.09$ **D** $\frac{1}{3} >$ 0.35

11. **Writing to Explain** Jayne says that 0.45 is greater than $\frac{4}{10}$. Is she correct?

    _____

    _____

    _____

Mixed Numbers and Decimals on the Number Line

Show each number on the number line.

1. $\frac{3}{10}$, $2\frac{3}{4}$, 2.8, 1.7

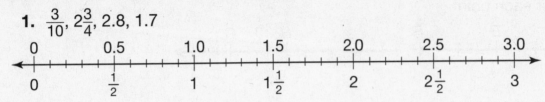

What point shows the location of each number?

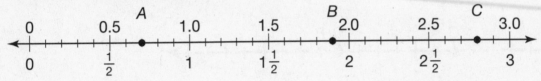

2. 1.9

_____

3. $\frac{7}{10}$

_____

4. $2\frac{8}{10}$

_____

5. Draw a number line to show the heights of each plant.

Plant Heights	
Seedling 1	$2\frac{3}{4}$ inches
Seedling 2	$3\frac{6}{10}$ inches
Seedling 3	2.8 inches
Seedling 4	3.4 inches

6. Which number is less than $3\frac{1}{2}$?

   A 3.7   **B** 3.6   **C** 3.5   **D** 3.4

7. **Writing to Explain** Last year, Mike grew 2.9 inches. Emily grew $2\frac{1}{4}$ inches. Who grew more?

   _____

Problem Solving:
Draw a Picture

Solve each problem. Write the answer in a complete sentence.

1. Three friends divided a veggie pizza into 12 slices. If they
    divide the pizza equally, what fraction of the pizza would
    each friend get?

    _____

2. Mark is making a quilt with his grandmother. Each row
    of the quilt has 6 squares. There are 8 rows. $\frac{1}{2}$ of the squares
    are blue. How many blue squares are in the quilt?

    _____

3. Jane pulled weeds in the garden 7 times. She was paid $5
    each time she pulled weeds for less than 1 hour and $6 each
    time she pulled weeds for more than 1 hour. If Jane received
    $39, how many times did she pull weeds for more than
    1 hour?

    _____

4. Neil needs to cut 3 long boards into 9 smaller
    boards. The first is 10 ft, the second is 16 ft, and
    the third is 18 ft. The table lists the smaller
    boards Neil needs. Use a drawing to show how
    he can divide the 3 boards so there is no waste.

Length of Board	Number Needed
4 ft	3
5 ft	4
6 ft	2

10 ft

16 ft

18 ft

Rounding Decimals

Round each decimal to the nearest whole number.

1 25.78 _____ **2.** 17.26 _____ **3.** 34.52 _____

4. 52.61 _____ **5.** 73.49 _____ **6.** 42.35 _____

7. 27.38 _____ **8.** 46.52 _____ **9.** 18.16 _____

Round each decimal to the nearest tenth.

10. 13.13 _____ **11.** 49.45 _____ **12.** 14.51 _____

13. 9.99 _____ **14.** 2.70 _____ **15.** 5.77 _____

16. 4.01 _____ **17.** 0.50 _____ **18.** 7.49 _____

19. When rounded to the nearest whole number, which decimals round to 9?

9.6   9.4   8.05   9.69   9.07   8.71   9.02   9.6   8.45

_____

20. When rounded to the nearest tenth, which decimals round to 3.8?

3.61   3.06   3.79   2.55   3.77   3.84   3.80   3.68

_____

21. Reasoning A swimmer's time in the 100-meter backstroke is
58 seconds when rounded to the nearest whole number. Name the fastest
and slowest times possible in decimals rounded to the hundredths place.

_____

22. Estimation It is 3.6 miles from Steve's house to the skating rink. Estimate the
distance from Steve's house to the skating rink.

A 3 miles   **B** 4 miles   **C** 5 miles   **D** 6 miles

23. Writing to Explain Round 8.95 to the nearest tenth. Did the
ones place change? Explain.

_____

_____

Estimating Sums and Differences of Decimals

Estimate each sum or difference.

1. 1.45 + 0.6 _____   **2.** 8.91 + 1.16 _____   **3.** 7.09 − 5.11 _____

4. 6.59 − 3.84 _____   **5.** 8.54 + 9.01 _____   **6.** 6.11 − 0.15 _____

7.   18.05   **8.**   11.45   **9.**   8.65   **10.**   9.50
      + 0.85   − 0.9   − 5.1   + 6.8

11. Reasoning Cheryl had $86.51. She bought 6 cases of fruit drink and had $50.67 left. About how much did Cheryl pay for each case of fruit drink?

12. Jean walked 19.87 mi last week, 17.15 mi the week before, and 18.92 mi this week. About how many miles has Jean walked in the 3 weeks?

_____

13. William drives 14.81 mi to work each day. Kathy drives 2.6 mi to work each day. About how much farther does William drive each day?

14. Which is the best estimate for the sum of 22.36 + 19.6?

    A 41   **B** 42   **C** 43   **D** 44

15. Writing to Explain Kayla needs $15.00 to buy a CD. She has $8.18 in her wallet, $3.19 in her pocket, and $5.42 in her piggy bank. Does Kayla have enough? Explain.

_____

_____

_____

_____

Modeling Addition and Subtraction of Decimals

Add or subtract. You may use grids to help.

1. 0.12 + 0.56 = _____

2. 0.27 − 0.09 = _____

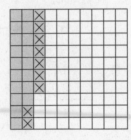

3. 0.86 + 0.54 = _____

4. 1.27 + 0.75 = _____

5. 0.93 − 0.25 = _____

6. 1.07 − 0.61 = _____

7. 1.13 − 1.02 = _____

8. 0.28 + 1.96 = _____

9. Number Sense Is the difference of
1.45 − 0.12 less than or greater than 1? _____

10. A bottle of nail polish holds 0.8 oz. A bottle of perfume
holds 0.45 oz. How many more ounces does a bottle
of nail polish hold? _____

11. Add: 1.18 + 1.86.

A 2.04   **B** 2.94   **C** 3.04   **D** 3.14

12. Writing to Explain Explain how you can use grids to
subtract 1.65 − 0.98.

_____

_____

_____

Adding and Subtracting Decimals

For **1** through **18**, add or subtract.

1. 6.33
  + 0.23

2. 37.41
  − 16.43

3. 15.19
  + 60.91

4. 2.67
  + 0.45

5. 66.34
  − 17.55

6. 68.33
  − 7.52

7. 54.08 − 45.81

8. 32.8 + 0.46

9. 54.28 − 17.7

10. 44.37 + 0.99

11. 14.19 − 12.14

12. 17.4 − 17.13

13. 8.27 + 7.84

14. 46.78 − 4.8

15. 17.66 − 12.79

16. 81.82 + 5.24

17. 61.22 − 33.82

18. 4.98 + 72.94

19. Christina walked 44.2 meters. She then walked 19.82 meters more. How many meters did she walk?

_____

20. Nelson has $18.82 in his left pocket. He has $14.33 in his right pocket. How much more money does he have in his left pocket?

A $4.44 **B** $4.49 **C** $4.51 **D** $4.59

21. Writing to Explain Explain why 4.2 + 0.2 is more than 4.2 + 0.12.

_____

_____

Multiplying a Whole Number by a Decimal

For **1** through **12**, multiply.

1. 1.2
$\times 2$

2. 2.7
$\times 3$

3. 6.4
$\times 6$

4. 12.1
$\times\ 2$

5. 24.6
$\times\ 5$

6. 39.2
$\times\ 8$

7. 17.4
$\times\ 9$

8. 61.0
$\times 11$

9. 3.57
$\times\ 2$

10. 6.49
$\times 12$

11. 18.12
$\times\ 23$

12. 20.05
$\times\ 5$

13. Mrs. Klein ran 2.5 miles on Saturday. Her husband ran 3 times more than she. How many miles did Mrs. Klein's husband run?

___

14. Susie sells 15 pencils for $0.10 each. How much money does she make?

A $150   **B** $15   **C** $1.50   **D** $0.15

15. Writing to Explain The ingredients for a recipe Cheryl is making cost $13.45. She needs to triple the recipe. She has $40. Does she have enough money for the ingredients? Explain.

___

___

___

Dividing a Decimal by a Whole Number

For **1** through **12**, divide.

1. 12.6 ÷ 6   **2.** 33.6 ÷ 3   **3.** 98.5 ÷ 5   **4.** 64.8 ÷ 4

_____   _____   _____   _____

5. 104.8 ÷ 2   **6.** 52.4 ÷ 4   **7.** 137.2 ÷ 7   **8.** 69.3 ÷ 3

_____   _____   _____   _____

9. 74.8 ÷ 4   **10.** 25.05 ÷ 5   **11.** 88.8 ÷ 6   **12.** 100.25 ÷ 5

_____   _____   _____   _____

13. Ari ran 16.4 miles in 4 hours at a steady pace. How many
miles did he run in an hour?

_____

14. Chico drank 32.5 ounces of water in 5 minutes. How many
ounces did he drink per minute?

A 7 oz   **B** 6.5 oz   **C** 6 oz   **D** 5.5 oz

15. Writing to Explain Sharon needs to make 5 uniforms for
the basketball team. She has a total of 12.5 giant spools of
thread. Each uniform requires 2.5 spools of thread. Does
Sharon have enough thread to make all the uniforms?
Explain.

_____

Problem Solving:
Try, Check, and Revise

Use the first try to help you make a second try. Finish solving the problem.

1. Mrs. Reid brought 32 orange and apple slices to her daughter's soccer practice. There were three times as many orange slices as there were apple slices. How many of each kind did she bring?

_____

Use the table to answer questions **2** through **4**.

2. Todd bought 2 items and spent $15.05. What did he buy?

_____

3. Sarah bought 4 items and spent $30.10. What did she buy?

Zeke's Toy Store	
Toy	**Cost**
Car	$5.55
Boat	$8.99
Train	$9.50

_____

4. Erin bought 3 items and spent $26.97. What did she buy?

_____

5. Greg has 5 coins in his pocket. The value of all 5 coins is $0.57. Which coins does he have in his pocket?

   A 1 quarter, 2 dimes, and 2 pennies   **C** 2 quarters, 1 nickel, and 2 pennies

   B 3 quarters and 2 pennies   **D** 2 quarters, 1 dime, and 2 pennies

6. **Writing to Explain** Jack has $2.00. What information do you need to find which coins he has?

_____

Understanding Area

For **1** through **4**, use the picture below.

Athletic Field

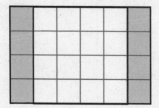

1. What is the area of the soccer section of the field? _____

2. What is the area of the field that is **NOT** being used? _____

3. How many square units of the athletic field are being used?

   _____

4. If the school used the soccer and baseball fields to build a football stadium, how large could the area of the stadium be?

   _____

5. What is the area of the shaded section?

   A 16 sq units   **B** 12 sq units   **C** 8 sq units   **D** 4 sq units

6. **Writing to Explain** A hexagon has a grid on it. The height of the hexagon is 2 units. What would be the approximate area? Explain.

   _____

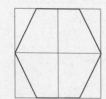

Area of Squares and Rectangles

Find the area of each figure.

1.
5 in.
5 in.

_____

2.
5 ft
9 ft

_____

3.

_____

4.
2 cm
2 cm
4 cm
6 cm
2 cm
4 cm
2 cm

_____

5. What is the area of both the bedrooms?

_____

6. What is the area of the whole house?

_____

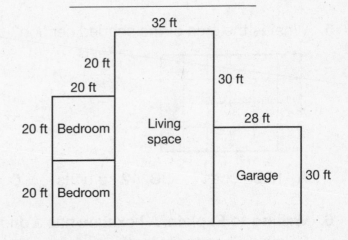

32 ft
20 ft
20 ft
20 ft Bedroom
Living space
30 ft
28 ft
20 ft Bedroom
Garage 30 ft

7. Which is the area of a rectangle with a length of 26 cm and a width of 34 cm?

  A 992 square cm **B** 884 square cm **C** 720 square cm **D** 324 square cm

8. **Writing to Explain** Explain how you would find the length of one side of a square if the area is 16 square units.

_____

Area of Irregular Shapes

Find the area of each shape.

1.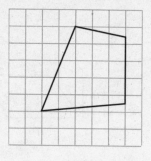

_____

2.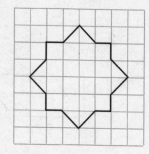

_____

3.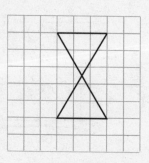

_____

4.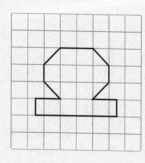

_____

5.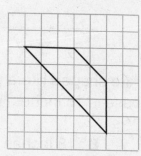

_____

6.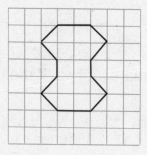

_____

7.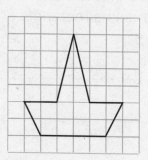

_____

8.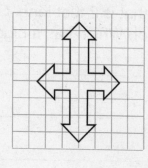

_____

Area of Parallelograms

Find the area of each of the following parallelograms in
1 through **8.**

1.

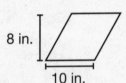

3 ft

4 ft

_____

2.

5 in.

9 in.

_____

3.

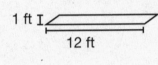

3 ft

3 ft

_____

4.

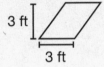

1 mi

2 mi

_____

5.

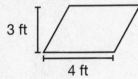

8 in.

10 in.

_____

6.

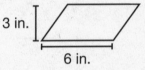

2 yd

3 yd

_____

7.

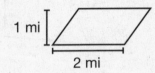

1 ft

12 ft

_____

8.

3 in.

6 in.

_____

9. The area of a kite shaped like a parallelogram is 324 square inches. If the
length of the base is 18 inches, what is the height?

   A 16 inches   **B** 18 inches   **C** 24 inches   **D** 28 inches

10. **Writing to Explain** Two parallelograms each have a side that is 3 feet long
and a height that is 2 feet long. One of the parallelograms is a rectangle and
the other is not. Which has a bigger area, and why?

_____

_____

_____

_____

Area of Triangles

Find the area of the triangles with these dimensions. You may draw a picture to help you.

1.

height: 10 ft

base: 10 ft

_____

2.

height: 20 ft

base: 4 ft

_____

3.

height: 3 ft

base: 20 ft

_____

4.

height: 3 ft

base: 8 ft

_____

5.

height: 11 ft

base: 14 ft

_____

6.

height: 71 ft

base: 10 ft

_____

7.

height: 2 ft

base: 100 ft

_____

8.

height: 4 ft

base: 50 ft

_____

9. Find the area of the triangle.

_____

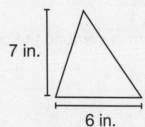

7 in.

6 in.

10. Which triangle has the smallest area?

A $B = 10$ ft, $h = 10$ ft

C $B = 24$ ft, $h = 3$ ft

B $B = 30$ ft, $h = 2$ ft

D $B = 40$ ft, $h = 1$ ft

11. Writing to Explain A square and a triangle have equal areas. If a side of the square is 10 inches and the base of the triangle is 10 inches, what is the height of the triangle? Explain. (Draw a diagram to solve the problem.)

_____

_____

_____

Perimeter

Find the perimeter of each figure.

1.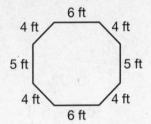

2.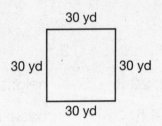

3.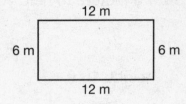

_____

_____

_____

4.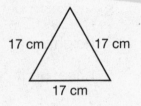

5.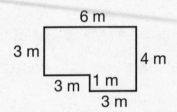

6.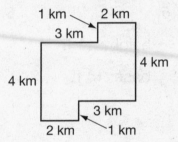

_____

_____

_____

7. What is the perimeter around the bases?

_____

8. Which is the perimeter of this figure?

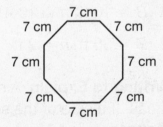

A 77 cm   **B** 63 cm

C 56 cm   **D** 28 cm

9. Writing to Explain Explain how you can use multiplication to find the perimeter of a square.

_____

_____

_____

_____

Same Perimeter, Different Area

For **1** through **9**, write "Yes" if the 2 rectangles have the same perimeter and "No" if they do not. If they have the same perimeter, tell which one has the greater area.

1.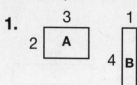

2.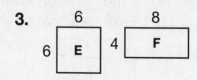

3.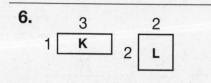

4.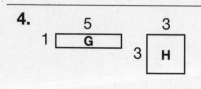

5.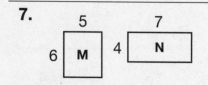

6.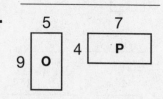

7.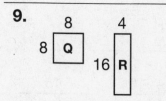

8.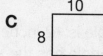

9.

10. Two rectangles have a perimeter of 16 inches. Name two possible areas for each rectangle.

_____

11. The length of a rectangle is 12 inches and the width is 6 inches. Which rectangle has the same perimeter?

A 6 ⌐⌐ 6

B 8 ⌐ 5

C 8 ⌐ 10

D 3 ⌐ 12

12. Writing to Explain The perimeter of rectangle Y is equal to its area. Rectangle Z has the same perimeter as rectangle Y. The length of rectangle Z is 5 inches and the width is 3 inches. Explain how you can find the length and width of rectangle Y.

_____

_____

_____

Same Area, Different Perimeter

For **1** through **9**, write "yes" if the 2 rectangles have the same area and "no" if they do not. If they have the same area, tell which one has the smaller perimeter.

1.   3   4
8 | A | 6 | B |

_____

2.   6   10
5 | C | 3 | D |

_____

3.   4   8
4 | E | 2 | F |

_____

4.   5   20
8 | G | 2 | H |

_____

5.   6   12
8 | I | 4 | J |

_____

6.   2   3
6 | K | 4 | L |

_____

7.   10   15
10 | M | 5 | N |

_____

8.   4   13
9 | O | 2 | P |

_____

9.   8   15
8 | Q | 1 | R |

_____

10. Two rectangles have an area of 81 square inches. Name two possible perimeters for the rectangles. _____

11. The length of a rectangle is 12 inches and the width is 12 inches. Which rectangle has the same area?

A   24
6 | |

C   13
11 | |

B   20
4 | |

D   48
2 | |

12. Writing to Explain The area of a rectangle is 100 square inches. The perimeter of the rectangle is 40 inches. A second rectangle has the same area but a different perimeter. Is the second rectangle a square? Explain why or why not.

_____

_____

Problem Solving:
Solve a Simpler Problem
and Make a Table

Sam needs to cut a piece of sheet metal into 8 pieces. It takes him 5 minutes to make each cut.

1. How many cuts will Sam make? _____

2. **Writing to Explain** How would making a table help you to find the number of minutes it took Sam to cut the sheet metal into 8 pieces?

   _____

   _____

3. How long will it take Sam to turn the sheet metal into 8 pieces? Write your answer in a complete sentence.

   _____

Sarah is having a slumber party with her 11 friends and they are telling scary stories. They divide into 3 groups and each group tells a story. Each group member talks for 3 minutes.

4. How many people are in each group? _____

5. How many minutes does each group take to tell a story? _____

6. How many minutes does it take for all three groups to tell their stories? _____

7. If Sarah divided her friends into 4 groups and each person still got the same time to talk, how long would it take to tell the stories?

   A 16 minutes   **B** 36 minutes   **C** 48 minutes   **D** 144 minutes

Solids

Complete the table.

Solid Figure	Number of Faces	Number of Edges	Number of Vertices
1. Square Pyramid			
2. Cube			
3. Triangular Prism			

Identify the solid figure that best describes each object.

4. _____

5. 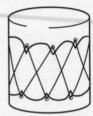 _____

6. 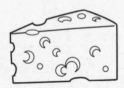 _____

7. How many total faces does a rectangular prism have? _____

8. Which solid does the figure represent?

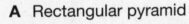

A Rectangular pyramid   **C** Rectangular prism

B Cylinder   **D** Square pyramid

9. Writing to Explain Explain the difference between a plane figure and a solid figure.

_____

_____

_____

Views of Solids: Nets

Solve.

1. What are the shapes of the faces of a triangular prism?

_____

2. What shape does a triangular prism have that a rectangular prism does not have?

_____

3. How many more vertices does a square pyramid have than a triangular pyramid?

_____

4. What shapes are the sides of a square pyramid?

_____

5. How many more vertices does a triangular prism have than a triangular pyramid?

_____

6. How many vertices does a rectangular prism have?

_____

7. What figure has 6 rectangles as faces?

_____

8. What figure has 2 triangular faces and 3 rectangular faces?

_____

9. How many more vertices does a rectangular prism have than a rectangular pyramid?

_____

10. Julie made a coin bank in the shape of a rectangular prism. She wants to paint each face a different color. How many colors will she need?

_____

11. Which solid figure has the most vertices?

A triangular prism

B rectangular prism

C rectangular pyramid

D triangular pyramid

12. Writing to Explain What is one difference between a prism and a pyramid?

_____

_____

_____

_____

Views of Solids: Perspective

For **1** through **9**, draw the perspective of the figure.

1. The top-down view of a rectangular pyramid

2. The side view of a rectangular pyramid

3. The top-down view of a cube

4. The side view of a cube

5. The top-down view of a triangular prism

6. The side view of a triangular prism

7. The top view of a rectangular prism

8. The side view of a rectangular prism

9. The side view of a triangular pyramid

10. Dennis and Ben want to build a square pyramid with blocks. They both draw a picture of it as it should appear from the side view. Dennis draws a square with a point in the middle. Ben draws a triangle. Whose drawing is accurate? _____

11. Which choice below gives the number of faces, edges, and vertices of a rectangular pyramid?

A 5, 8, 5   **B** 4, 7, 4   **C** 6, 12, 8   **D** 8, 10, 8

12. Writing to Explain What is the difference between the shape of a side view of a rectangular pyramid and a top-down view of a rectangular pyramid?

_____

_____

Volume

Compute the volume of these figures:

1. A pool 44 feet by 9 feet by 8 feet

2. A loaf of bread 6 inches by 18 inches by 6 inches

3. A room 6 feet by 8 feet by 9 feet

4. A room 3 yards by 9 yards by 10 yards

_____   _____   _____   _____

5. A CD case 4 inches by 4 inches by $\frac{1}{4}$ inch

6. A book that is 10 inches by 14 inches by 3 inches

7. A briefcase 2 feet by 1 foot by $\frac{1}{2}$ foot

8. A box of lead which is 1 foot by 1 foot by 1 foot

_____   _____   _____   _____

9. Find the volume of a cube with a height of 3 feet. _____

10. A wall is built of large blocks that are 1 foot by 1 foot by 1 foot, and each weigh 100 pounds. The volume of the wall is 240 cubic feet. What is the weight of the wall?

A 100 lb   **B** 240 lb   **C** 24,000 lb   **D** 240,000 lb

11. **Writing to Explain** A box that is 10 inches tall, 8 inches wide, and 2 inches deep is filled with blocks that are 2 inches by 2 inches by 2 inches. Can 20 blocks fit into the box? Explain. (Hint: Draw a diagram to solve the problem.)

_____

_____

_____

_____

Problem Solving:
Look for a Pattern

Look for a pattern. Draw the next two shapes.

1.

2.

Look for a pattern. Write the missing numbers.

3. 5, 8, 11, 14, 17, _____ , _____

4. 4, 6, 10, 16, 24, _____ , _____

Look for a pattern. Complete each number sentence.

5. $80 + 8 = 88$

    $808 + 80 = 888$

    $8,008 + 880 =$ _____

    $80,808 + 8,080 =$ _____

6. $10 + 1 = 11$

    $100 + 1 = 101$

    $1,000 + 1 =$ _____

    $10,000 + 1 =$ _____

Look for a pattern. Write the missing numbers.

7. Sally went to purchase tiles for her kitchen floor. She measured the floor to find how many tiles she needed to cover the floor. Sally decided to make a pattern. She chose 10 red tiles, 20 beige tiles, 30 white tiles, _____ black tiles, and _____ gray tiles to complete a pattern for the kitchen floor.

8. **Reasoning** Fill in the missing amounts to update Carl's savings account.

Carl's Savings Account

Date	Deposit	Balance
4/7	$25	$945
4/14		$995
4/21	$25	
4/30	$50	
5/7		$1,095

Customary Units of Length

Choose the most appropriate unit to measure the length of each. Write in., ft, yd, or mi.

1. boat _____

2. wallet _____

3. soccer field _____

4. finger bandage _____

5. computer cable _____

6. train route _____

7. nose _____

8. sea _____

Estimate first. Then, measure each length to the nearest inch.

9. |———————————————| _____

10. |———————| _____

11. Use a ruler to find the length of one side of the triangle. Then find the perimeter.

_____

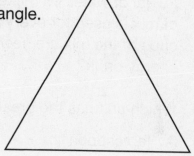

12. Eileen needs 9 feet of fabric to make a skirt. If Eileen has 18 feet of fabric how many skirts can she make?

_____

13. Which unit would be most appropriate for measuring the length of a barn?

A inches   **B** pounds   **C** yards   **D** miles

14. Writing to Explain Explain how you would decide which unit is best for measuring your math book.

_____

_____

Customary Units of Capacity

Choose the most appropriate unit or units to measure the
capacity of each. Write tsp, tbsp, fl oz, c, pt, qt, or gal.

1. teacup   _____   2. juice box   _____

3. motor oil   _____   4. chicken stock
                                        in a recipe   _____

5. carton of cream _____   6. lake   _____

7. **Number Sense** Would a teaspoon be a good way to
   measure the capacity of a milk carton? Explain.

   _____

   _____

8. A refreshment jug for the baseball team holds
   20 gal of water. To make an energy drink, 1 c
   of mix is used for every 2 gal of water. How many
   cups of the mix are needed to fill the jug with
   energy drink?   _____

9. Which unit has the greatest capacity?

   A Tablespoon   **C** Pint

   B Quart   **D** Teaspoon

10. **Writing to Explain** Cassidy says that capacity is the same
    as the amount. Do you agree? Explain why or why not.

    _____

    _____

    _____

    _____

Units of Weight

Choose the most appropriate unit to measure the weight of each.
Write oz, lb, or T.

1. truck _____ 2. can of vegetables _____

3. person _____ 4. desk _____

5. trailer full of bricks _____ 6. cup of flour _____

7. box of paper _____ 8. CD _____

9. **Reasoning** Would a scale that is used to weigh food be the
   best tool to weigh concrete blocks? Explain why or why not.

   _____

   _____

   _____

10. Jen wants to weigh her cat. Should she weigh the
    cat with ounces, pounds, or tons? _____

11. What unit would you use to measure the weight of
    your house? _____

12. Which animal would it be appropriate to measure in ounces?

    A mouse   **B** elephant   **C** horse   **D** cow

13. **Writing to Explain** Dezi says that there are more ounces
    in 1 T than there are pounds. Do you agree? Explain.

    _____

    _____

    _____

Changing Customary Units

For **1** through **12**, compare. Write $>$, $<$, or $=$ for each $\bigcirc$.

1. 1 yd $\bigcirc$ 4 ft

2. 40 in. $\bigcirc$ 1 yd

3. 6 pt $\bigcirc$ 3 qt

4. 3 lb $\bigcirc$ 50 oz

5. 2 yd $\bigcirc$ 6 ft

6. 3 ft $\bigcirc$ 30 in.

7. 1 gal $\bigcirc$ 15 c

8. 3 T $\bigcirc$ 3,000 lb

9. 1 mi $\bigcirc$ 2,000 yd

10. 100 ft $\bigcirc$ 100 mi

11. 1 gal $\bigcirc$ 100 fl oz

12. 3 tbsp $\bigcirc$ 10 tsp

13. Which measurement is **NOT** equal to 1 mile?

    A 1,760 yd   **B** 5,280 yd   **C** 5,280 ft   **D** 63,360 in.

14. Writing to Explain A recipe calls for 4 tsp of baking soda and 1 fl oz of vanilla. Which measurement is greater? Explain.

_____

_____

_____

Using Metric Units of Length

Choose the most appropriate unit to measure each. Write mm,
cm, dm, m, or km.

1. width of a house

_____

2. distance across Lake Erie

_____

3. width of a thumbtack

_____

4. thickness of a phone book

_____

Estimate first. Then, find each length to the nearest
centimeter.

5. ⊢————————⊣

_____ , _____

6. ⊢————⊣

_____ , _____

7. **Number Sense** Which would you be more
likely to measure in centimeters, a fish tank
or a swimming pool?

_____

8. Which is longer, a 12 cm pencil or a 1 dm pen? _____

9. Which is the most appropriate measure for the length of a skateboard?

A 5 mm   **B** 5 cm   **C** 5 dm   **D** 5 m

10. **Writing to Explain** Jill measured the length of her eraser.
She wrote 5 on her paper without the unit. Which metric
unit of measure should Jill include?

_____

_____

_____

Metric Units of Capacity

Choose the most appropriate unit to measure the capacity of each. Write L or mL.

1. water in a bathtub

2. perfume in a bottle

3. soup in a can

_____ _____ _____

4. **Number Sense** Which will be less, the number of liters or the number of milliliters, of water in a pool? _____

5. Name something you might measure in liters.

_____

6. Name something you might measure in milliliters.

_____

7. A gallon of milk is the same as 3.78 L of milk. How many liters of milk are there in 2 gal? _____

8. A small can of tomato juice contains 56.8 mL of juice. A large can of tomato juice contains 202.62 mL of juice. How much juice is there in the large and small can combined? _____

9. Which capacity would you be most likely to measure in milliliters?

    A gas in a car

    C tea in a cup

    B water in a lake

    D detergent in a bottle

10. **Writing to Explain** Would you be more likely to measure the amount of water in your kitchen sink in liters or milliliters? Explain.

_____

_____

Units of Mass

Choose the most appropriate unit to measure the mass of each.
Write g or kg.

1. banana _____

2. tractor _____

3. coin _____

4. bowling ball _____

5. letter _____

6. encyclopedia _____

7. **Number Sense** Which is a greater number, the mass of a
cat in grams or the mass of the same cat in kilograms?

_____

8. The *Dromornis stirtoni* was once the largest
living bird. It is now extinct. The ostrich is
now the largest living bird. What is the
difference in mass between the *Dromornis
stirtoni* and the ostrich?

Bird	Mass
Ostrich	156 kg
Andean condor	9 kg
Eurasian eagle owl	4.2 kg
Dromornis stirtoni	454 kg

_____

9. Which has a larger mass, an Andean condor or a Eurasian
eagle owl?

_____

10. Which object would be most likely to have a mass of 2 kg?

    A A truck   **B** An orange   **C** A mosquito   **D** A math book

11. **Writing to Explain** Would you be more likely to find the
mass of a pen in grams or in kilograms? Explain.

_____

_____

_____

Changing Metric Units

For **1** through **12**, compare. Write >, <, for each ◯.

1. 4 m ◯ 400 dm

2. 4 dm ◯ 40 cm

3. 10 L ◯ 1,000 mL

4. 2 kg ◯ 1,500 g

5. 15 cm ◯ 150 mm

6. 1 km ◯ 999 m

7. 4 L ◯ 4,500 mL

8. 500 g ◯ 5 kg

9. 6 km ◯ 6,000 m

10. 200 cm ◯ 3 m

11. 3,000 m ◯ 2 km

12. 100 mm ◯ 1 dm

13. Which measurement is **NOT** equal to 3 m?

A 30 dm   **B** 300 cm   **C** 3,000 mm   **D** 3,000 cm

14. Writing to Explain If 5 potatoes together weigh a kilogram
and 8 pears together weigh 1,200 grams, which weighs
more, a potato or a pear? Explain.

_____

_____

_____

Units of Time

Write >, <, or = for each ◯.

1. 48 hours ◯ 4 days

2. 1 year ◯ 12 months

3. 60 minutes ◯ 2 hours

4. 17 days ◯ 2 weeks

5. 5 months ◯ 40 weeks

6. 1 millennium ◯ 10 centuries

7. 6 decades ◯ 1 century

8. 5 decades ◯ 48 years

9. Cheryl's grandparents have been married for 6 decades. How many years have they been married?

_____

10. Tom was in elementary school from 1997 to 2002. How much time was that in years?

_____

The Declaration of Independence was signed on July 4, 1776. The United States celebrated the bicentennial on July 4, 1976. How much time was that in

11. years? _____

12. decades? _____

13. 49 days = ☐

A 5 weeks **B** 6 weeks **C** 7 weeks **D** 8 weeks

14. Writing to Explain Which is longer: 180 sec or 3 min? Explain how you decided.

_____

_____

_____

Elapsed Time

Find each elapsed time.

1. Start: 3:52 P.M.
Finish: 4:10 P.M.

_____

2. Start: 11:35 A.M.
Finish: 12:25 P.M.

_____

3. Start: 3:15 P.M.
Finish: 5:00 P.M.

_____

4. Start: 8:20 A.M.
Finish: 2:35 P.M.

_____

Write the time each clock will show in 30 min.

5.

_____

6.

_____

7.

_____

8. Number Sense Max says that the elapsed time from
11:55 A.M. to 1:10 P.M. is more than an hour and a half.
Is he correct? Explain.

_____

_____

9. Gary began eating lunch at 12:17 P.M. and finished at
1:01 P.M. Which is the elapsed time?

A 41 min   **B** 42 min   **C** 43 min   **D** 44 min

10. Writing to Explain Ella went in the swimming pool at
1:20 P.M. She swam for 1 hour 20 minutes. What time was it
when she finished swimming? Show your work.

_____

_____

Temperature

For problems **1** through **12**, compute the change in temperature.
Tell whether it is an increase or decrease.

1. From 18°F to 45°F	2. From 65°F to 40°F	3. From 10°C to 0°C	4. From 25°C to 45°C
5. From 37°C to 10°C	6. From 0°C to 100°C	7. From 32°F to 212°F	8. From 85°F to 58°F
9. From 24.5°C to 36.8°C	10. From 98.6°F to 102.1°F	11. From 99°F to 94.6°F	12. From 8.2°C to 1.4°C

13. The temperature during a heat wave was 98°F. After a thunderstorm, the temperature was 62°F. What was the change in temperature?

   A 36°F decrease   **B** 36°F increase   **C** 62°F decrease   **D** 98°F increase

14. **Writing to Explain** Water freezes at 32°F and 0°C. Water boils at 212°F and 100°C. Which measures a bigger heat change, 1°C or 1°F?

   _____

   _____

   _____

Problem Solving:
Work Backward

Solve by working backward. Write the answer in a complete sentence.

1. There were 21 students in Travis's fourth-grade class at the end of the school year. During the year four new students joined his class, and 2 moved away. One student was transferred to another fourth-grade teacher. How many students were in Travis's class at the beginning of the school year?

_____

_____

_____

2. Sir John Franklin was an explorer who traveled in Canada and the United States. He was 33 years old when he began exploring northwestern Canada. In a second expedition 17 years later, he explored as far as Alaska. 11 years later, Franklin died in an expedition in search of a Northwest Passage in 1847. In what year was Franklin born?

_____

3. Tessie has a volleyball game at 7:00 P.M. She needs to be there 20 minutes early to warm up for the game, and it takes her 45 minutes to get to the gym. What time should she leave her house?

_____

4. Frank bought lunch for $5.60 at a diner. He spent $2.00 to ride the bus to the mall and back, and spent $6.50 while he was at the mall. His friend Bill paid him back $5.00 that he had borrowed last week. If Frank arrived at home with $10.50 in his pocket, how much did he have when he left home that morning?

_____

Data from Surveys

Use the data in the tally chart.

Favorite Frozen Yogurt	
Banana	|||
Blueberry	~~||||~~ ~~||||~~ ||
Strawberry	~~||||~~
Vanilla	~~||||~~ |||

1. How many people in the survey liked strawberry-flavored frozen yogurt best?

   _____

2. Which flavor of frozen yogurt received the most votes?

   _____

3. How many people liked vanilla frozen yogurt best?

   _____

4. How many people were surveyed?

   _____

5. **Number Sense** Could the frozen yogurt survey help restaurants choose flavors of frozen yogurt? Explain.

   _____

   _____

   _____

6. Which is the last step in taking a survey?

   A Explain the results   **C** Count tallies

   B Write a survey question   **D** Make a tally chart and
        ask the question

7. **Writing to Explain** Give an example of a topic for a survey question in which the results for the answers could be similar.

   _____

   _____

   _____

Interpreting Graphs

Free-Throw Shots

1. How many free-throw shots did
   Jan make?

   _____

2. How many free-throw shots did
   Bob make?

   _____

3. Who made 35 free-throw shots?

   _____

4. Who made 15 free-throw shots?

   _____

5. **Number Sense** How can you easily tell who completed
   about the same number of free-throw shots?

   _____

   _____

6. What are the numbers that show the units on a graph called?

   A Scale   **B** Intervals   **C** Horizontal axis   **D** Vertical axis

7. **Writing to Explain** Describe the interval you would use for
   a bar graph if the data ranges from 12 to 39 units.

   _____

   _____

   _____

Line Plots

Number of Rabbits in Each Litter	1	2	3	4	5	6	7	8	9	10	11	12
Litters	/	///	###	### ////	### ###	### ///	////	////	///	###	///	/

1. Make a line plot of the number of rabbits in each litter.

   a. Write a label at the bottom.

   b. Put Xs on the number line to show the number of rabbits in a litter.

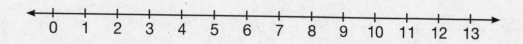

```
←──┼──┼──┼──┼──┼──┼──┼──┼──┼──┼──┼──┼──┼──→
   0  1  2  3  4  5  6  7  8  9  10 11 12 13
```

2. How many Xs are shown for 6? _____

3. What is the number of rabbits that appears in a litter most often?

   A 3 rabbits   **B** 4 rabbits   **C** 5 rabbits   **D** 6 rabbits

4. **Writing to Explain** Is the 1-rabbit litter an outlier?

   _____

   _____

Ordered Pairs

For **1** through **5**, write the ordered pair for each point.

1. P _____

2. R _____

3. S _____

4. U _____

5. X _____

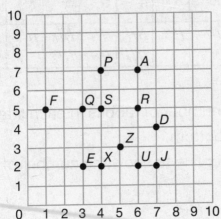

For **6** through **10**, name the point for each ordered pair.

6. (7, 4) _____

7. (3, 2) _____

8. (1, 5) _____

9. (7, 2) _____

10. (6, 7) _____

11. What point is at (3, 5)?
   A Point *Z*   **B** Point *Q*   **C** Point *S*   **D** Point *R*

12. **Writing to Explain** Doug is standing at (2, 1). Susan is standing at (1, 2). Who is farther to the right? How do you know?

_____

Line Graphs

Use the line graph for Exercises **1** through **6**.

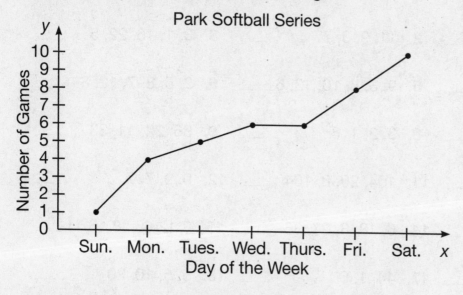

Park Softball Series

1. On which day(s) were the fewest games played? _____

2. How many games were played during the entire week? _____

3. Between which two days was there no increase or decrease

    in the number of games played? _____

4. Is this graph a good way to show which team won the series? Explain.

    _____

5. How many games were played on Monday?

    A 2 games   **B** 3 games   **C** 4 games   **D** 5 games

6. **Writing to Explain** Between which two days was there the greatest increase
    in games played?

    _____

    _____

    _____

Mean

In Exercises **1** through **18**, find the mean of each group.

1. 6, 2, 4, 8 _____   **2.** 11, 9, 3, 77 _____   **3.** 6, 1, 16, 22, 5 _____

4. 12, 13, 17 _____   **5.** 9, 3, 8, 10, 12, 6 _____   **6.** 2, 5, 8, 7, 12, 8 _____

7. 6, 9, 101, 4 _____   **8.** 3, 2, 1, 6 _____   **9.** 66, 22, 11, 33 _____

10. 53, 22, 16, 61, 73 _____   **11.** 104, 20, 8, 104 _____   **12.** 9, 9, 7, 7 _____

13. 22, 23, 24, 35 _____   **14.** 6, 18, 3, 27, 36 _____   **15.** 3, 12, 66, 18, 16, 11 _____

16. 4, 3, 4, 5 _____   **17.** 44, 1, 6 _____   **18.** 5, 5, 10, 20 _____

19. Donald scored a 99 on a test. Two of his friends scored a 97 and one of his

friends scored a 95. What is the mean of their scores? _____

20. Liz caught 8 fish at the lake. Jay caught 4 fish. What is the mean number

of fish they caught if Jay catches 2 more fish? _____

21. Michelle is 57 inches tall. Her older sister is 65 inches tall, and her younger
brother is 46 inches tall. What is the mean of their heights?

A 46 inches   **B** 54 inches   **C** 56 inches   **D** 62 inches

22. **Writing to Explain** The mean score for a test is 88. One
more score is added to the data. Explain if it is possible for
the mean to remain 88.

_____

_____

Median, Mode, and Range

In Exercises **1** through **9**, find the median, mode, and range of each set of data.

1. 48, 11, 15, 14, 11

median: _____

mode: _____

range: _____

2. 3, 9, 3, 11, 23, 15, 15, 12, 3, 9, 14

median: _____

mode: _____

range: _____

3. 5, 2, 1, 1, 3, 7, 6

median: _____

mode: _____

range: _____

4. 17, 13, 12, 18, 17, 10, 27

median: _____

mode: _____

range: _____

5. 33, 44, 55, 22, 55, 11, 66

median: _____

mode: _____

range: _____

6. 21, 63, 22, 18, 35, 29, 63

median: _____

mode: _____

range: _____

7. 17, 47, 12, 13, 12

median: _____

mode: _____

range: _____

8. 2, 8, 24, 12, 22, 62, 61, 62, 82

median: _____

mode: _____

range: _____

9. 19, 16, 55, 25, 16, 21, 19

median: _____

mode: _____

range: _____

Use the table below for Execises **10** and **11**.

Person	Amy	Bob	Clair	Dave	Erin	Frank	Gina
Hours	7	7	2	4	8	5	6

10. Amy determined the number of hours her classmates volunteer each month. Name all the people who volunteer for more than the median of the data.

_____

11. Which person volunteered an amount of time equal to the range?

A Amy   **B** Clair   **C** Dave   **D** Gina

12. Writing to Explain The median score on a test is 90. Is it possible to add two more scores to the data and still have a median score of 90? Explain.

_____

_____

_____

Stem-and-Leaf Plots

For Exercises **1** through **4** use the following plot.

Stem	Leaf
0	3, 3, 3, 7, 8, 8
1	1, 1, 3, 4, 5, 7, 8, 9
2	1, 3, 3, 5, 7, 8, 9

1. What numbers are listed in the stem-and-leaf plot above?

_____

_____

2. What is the median of the values? _____

3. What is the mode of the values? _____

4. What is the range of the values? _____

For Exercises **5** through **9** use the following plot.

Stem	Leaf
7	
8	1, 2, 5, 5, 5, 8
9	0, 1, 3

5. What numbers are listed in the stem-and-leaf plot above?

_____

6. What is the mode of the values? _____

7. What is the range of the values? _____

8. What is the median of the values?

    A 85   **B** 88   **C** 91   **D** 100

9. **Writing to Explain** What does it mean if there isn't a leaf when there is a stem of 7?

_____

Reading a Circle Graph

Use the circle graph to answer Exercises **1** through **7**.

Language spoken at home

1. In simplest form, what fraction of
   people speak Spanish at home?   _____

2. In simplest form, what fraction of
   people speak English at home?   _____

3. In simplest form, what fraction of
   people speak Japanese at home?   _____

4. In simplest form, what fraction of people do
   NOT speak either Chinese or Japanese at home? _____

5. In simplest form, what fraction of people
   do **NOT** speak English at home?   _____

6. If 20 people were surveyed, then how many people speak
   either English or Spanish at home?

   A 6   **B** 8   **C** 14   **D** 20

7. **Writing to Explain** Why can't you use this graph to find out if someone
   speaks both English and Chinese at home?

   _____

   _____

   _____

Problem Solving: Make a Graph

Complete the graph to solve each problem.

1.

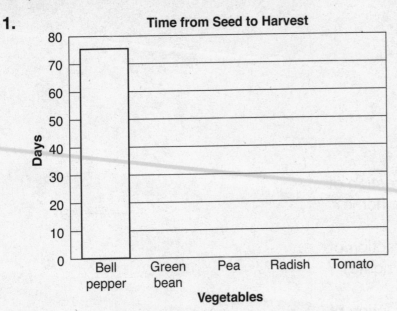

Time from Seed to Harvest

Vegetable	Days
Bell pepper	75
Green bean	56
Pea	75
Radish	23
Tomato	73

2. Which vegetables take the greatest amount of time to harvest? How much greater is this number of days than the number of days needed to harvest radishes?

_____

_____

3. Which vegetable plant will be ready to harvest earlier, the bell pepper plant or the tomato plant? How many days earlier?

_____

4. **Number Sense** Which vegetable plants will be ready to harvest within 5 days of the tomato plant?

_____

5. Write the missing numbers.   7, 10, 13, 16, _____, _____, _____

Equal or Not Equal

Answer each question. Tell why or why not.

	You know:	Does:
1.	$61 + 27 = 88$	$61 + 27 - 8 = 88 \times 8$?
2.	$76 - 59 = 17$	$(76 - 59) + 12 = 17 - 12$?
3.	$24 \times 6 = 144$	$(24 \times 6) - 72 = 144 - 72$?

	Given the equation:	Does:
4.	$15 \times w = 105$	$15 \times w + 51 = 105 + 51$?
5.	$57 + x = 202$	$57 + x - 13 = 202 - 13$?
6.	$w + 9 = 27$	$(w + 9) \times 4 = 27 + 4$?

7. What could you do to the equation $40 \times y = 320$ to keep the sides equal?

   A $(40 \times y) \times 2 = 320 \times 2$

   B $(40 \times y) + 3 = 320 - 3$

   C $(40 \times y) \div 8 = 320 - 8$

   D $(40 \times y) + 12 = 320 + 18$

8. Writing to Explain If you start with an unbalanced scale and add the same amount to each side, what happens to the scale?

_____

_____

Solving Addition and Subtraction Equations

For Exercises **1** and **2**, solve for each ☐.

1. $w - 8 = 26$

$w - 8 + \boxed{} = 26 + \boxed{}$

$w = \boxed{}$

2. $r + 11 = 19$

$r + 11 - \boxed{} = 19 - \boxed{}$

$r = \boxed{}$

For Exercises **3** through **14**, solve each equation.

3. $k + 4 = 21$ _____

4. $j - 7 = 6$ _____

5. $q - 2 = 39$ _____

6. $h + 350 = 450$ _____

7. $b - 44 = 6$ _____

8. $t + 52 = 61$ _____

9. $e - 28 = 44$ _____

10. $n + 63 = 108$ _____

11. $p + 7 = 111$ _____

12. $64 - s = 25$ _____

13. $c - 71 = 18$ _____

14. $z - 13 = 13$ _____

15. Ben walked 8 miles to a friend's house and 4 more miles to the park. Write and solve an equation to show how many miles Ben walked.

_____

16. Carla made 27 gift baskets. She has given 8 away. Which equation shows how to find the number of gift baskets Carla has left?

A $8 + 27 = b$ **B** $b + 27 = 8$ **C** $b - 27 = 8$ **D** $27 - 8 = b$

17. Writing to Explain Roger knows how many keys a piano has. He knows that some of the keys are broken. How can he find the number of keys that work?

_____

_____

_____

Solving Multiplication and Division Equations

Solve each equation.

1. $q \times 9 = 18$ _____
2. $99 \div e = 33$ _____
3. $k \times 4 = 48$ _____

4. $y \div 8 = 9$ _____
5. $7 \times w = 42$ _____
6. $y \times 5 = 65$ _____

7. $b \div 7 = 7$ _____
8. $54 \div a = 6$ _____
9. $u \div 3 = 18$ _____

10. $2 \times t = 2$ _____
11. $x \div 6 = 8$ _____
12. $7 \times r = 21$ _____

13. $m \div 8 = 7$ _____
14. $v \times 8 = 96$ _____
15. $e \times 4 = 68$ _____

16. Kyle spent 3 hours each day for 4 days making up a song. Write and solve an equation to find the number of total hours Kyle spent making up his song.

_____

17. Liz played hockey for 28 hours last week. She played for an equal amount of time for 7 days. Write and solve an equation to find the number of hours Liz played hockey for each day.

_____

18. Vincent worked 9 hours each day for 8 days. Write and solve an equation to find the total number of hours Vincent worked.

_____

19. Veronica reads 9 pages in a book each day. The book is 216 pages long. Which equation shows how to find the number of days it will take Veronica to read the book?

A $b \div 9 = 216$

C $9 \times 216 = b$

B $b \div 216 = 9$

D $216 \div 9 = b$

20. **Writing to Explain** Alexandra has 18 yo-yos. She spent $9.00 to buy them all. She wrote the equation $18 \div 9 = y$ to find how many yo-yos she got for each dollar she spent. Sven has 9 yo-yos. He spent $18.00 to buy them all. He wrote the equation $18 \div 9 = y$. What does Sven's equation tell him?

_____

Understanding Inequalities

Give 3 values that solve the inequality for problems **1** through **16**.

1. $x > 0$ **2.** $y > 5$ **3.** $z < 10$ **4.** $z < 3$

_____   _____   _____   _____

5. $x > 4$ **6.** $x < 4$ **7.** $x > 170$ **8.** $x > 1$

_____   _____   _____   _____

9. $x < 9$ **10.** $x < 6$ **11.** $y > 2$ **12.** $y > 100$

_____   _____   _____   _____

13. $z < 8$ **14.** $x > 77$ **15.** $u > 10.9$ **16.** $u < 13.99$

_____   _____   _____   _____

17. Draw the inequality $x < 7$ on a number line.

18. Draw the inequality $x > 7$ on a number line.

19. Which is **NOT** a solution to $x > 18$?

   A 18   **B** 18.000001   **C** 19   **D** 30

20. **Writing to Explain** Is 0 a solution to $x > 0$? Why or why not?

_____

_____

Problem Solving:
Work Backward

Work backward to help you solve each exercise.

1. Jenny is training for a race. On Day 1, she ran 5 miles, which was $\frac{1}{3}$ the distance she ran on Day 3, and $\frac{1}{2}$ the distance she ran on Day 2. How many miles did she run over the 3-day period?

   _____

2. In June 2000, a sixth-grade class planted a tree in the schoolyard. The tree grew about 3 inches a year. If the tree was 38 inches high in June 2005, about how high was the tree when it was planted?

   _____

3. Sean is 4 months older than Tony. Heather is 6 months younger than Tony. If Sean's birthday is in April, in which months are Heather's and Tony's birthdays?

   _____

4. Joe made a frozen yogurt shake with 10 ounces of milk and some strawberry frozen yogurt. He used the mixture to fill three 5-ounce glasses and had 2 ounces left over. How much frozen yogurt did he use?

   _____

5. The debate club members sold raffle tickets to raise money for T-shirts. They sold 3 times as many raffle tickets on the weekend as they did during the week. On the weekend, they sold 246 tickets. How many raffle tickets did they sell during the week?

   _____

Name _____

Translations

A translation moves a figure up, down, left, or right.

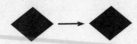

When a figure is translated, the size and the shape of the figure does not change.

Tell if the figures are related by translation.

1.

_____

2.

_____

3.

_____

4.

_____

5.

_____

6.

_____

7. Writing to Explain Can a translation make a figure larger or smaller?

_____

8. Which is a translation of the figure?

A

B

C

D

Reflections

A reflection is the mirror image of a figure that has been flipped over a line.

A reflection of a figure does not change the figure's size or shape.

Tell if the figures are related by a reflection.

1.

_____

2.

_____

3.

_____

4.

_____

5.

_____

6.

_____

7. Writing to Explain Look at the s-shapes on the violin. Are they related by a reflection? Explain your answer.

_____

_____

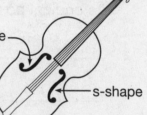

s-shape

s-shape

8. Which choice is a reflection?

A

B

C

D

Name _____

Rotations

A rotation is the way a figure moves around a point, or turns.
A rotation never changes the shape or size of the figure.

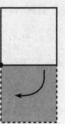

Are the figures related by rotation?

1.

2.

3.

_____

_____

_____

4.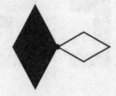

5.

6.

_____

_____

_____

7. Writing to Explain How can four turns put a figure back in
its original position?

_____

_____

_____

_____

Congruent Figures

Congruent figures have the same size and shape, although they
may face different directions.

Tell if the figures are congruent.

1.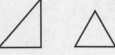

2.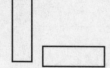

3.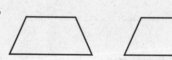

_____

4.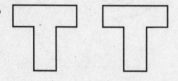

5.

6.

_____

7. Writing to Explain If you divide a 4 in. by 8 in. rectangle
from corner to corner, what new shapes do you get? Are they
congruent? Why or why not?

_____

_____

_____

_____

Line Symmetry

Tell if each line is a line of symmetry.

1.

_____

2.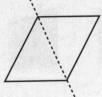

_____

3.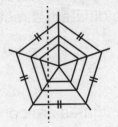

_____

Tell how many lines of symmetry each figure has.

4.

_____

5.

_____

6.

_____

7. Draw lines of symmetry.

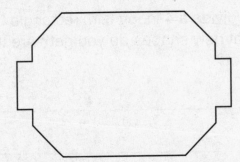

8. How many lines of symmetry does a rhombus that is not a square have?

  A 0   **B** 1   **C** 2   **D** 3

9. Writing to Explain Explain why a square is always symmetric.

_____

_____

Rotational Symmetry

Tell if the figure has rotational symmetry. Write yes or no.

1.

_____

2.

_____

3.

_____

4.

_____

5.

_____

6.

_____

7.

_____

8.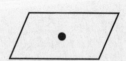

_____

9. Which figure has rotational symmetry?

A   B   C   D

10. **Writing to Explain** Which figure, a square or a trapezoid, will
rotate onto itself in 90°? Explain.

_____

_____

_____

Name _____

Problem Solving:
Draw a Picture

Kacey is making a necklace that is 16 inches long. She uses
5 beads for every inch. How many beads will she need?

1. **Writing to Explain** Draw a picture and explain how it can
   help to solve.

   _____

   _____

   _____

2. Write a number sentence based on the picture you drew.

   _____

3. How many beads will Kacey need? _____

4. Explain how you can check your answer.

   _____

   _____

Roger has a 64-inch piece of wood he needs to cut into 8 pieces.

5. How many cuts does Roger need to make? _____

6. **Writing to Explain** For Exercise **5**, how did drawing a picture
   help you solve the problem?

   _____

   _____

7. Write a number sentence and solve for how long each piece
   of board will be if each piece is an equal length.

   _____

Finding Combinations

Show the possible combinations by filling in the table.

1.

Mark	✔	✚	✘
Shape	●	■	▲

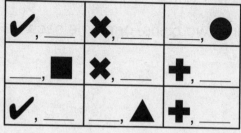

For **2** through **5**, find the number of possible combinations. Draw
a picture or use objects to help you.

2. Choose one of 3 soups and one
   of 2 salads.

   _____

3. Choose one of 4 cups and one
   of 2 juices.

   _____

4. Choose one of 5 paints and one
   of 3 trims.

   _____

5. Choose one of 7 shirts and one
   of 3 pants.

   _____

6. **Reasoning** June has 1 coat and
   7 scarves. How many combinations
   of coats and scarves does she have? _____

7. Ross has 3 ties and 4 dress shirts. How many possible
   combinations of ties and dress shirts does he have?

   A 3   **B** 4   **C** 12   **D** 21

8. **Writing to Explain** Carl has 1 kind of bread, crunchy and smooth
   peanut butter, and several kinds of jellies. What information do
   you need to find the number of possible combinations of peanut
   butter and jelly sandwiches he can make?

   _____

Outcomes and Tree Diagrams

A coin has two sides, heads and tails. Make a tree diagram to list
all the possible outcomes for each situation.

1. Flipping two coins, one time each

2. Flipping three coins, one time each

3. A deli offers lunch sandwiches for $1.00 with a choice
   of two cheeses and three meats. How many possible sandwich
   combinations of one meat and one cheese are there?

   _____

4. **Reasoning** A number cube with the numbers 1, 2, 3, 4, 5, and 6
   is tossed two times. Is it likely, unlikely, certain, or impossible for
   the same number to be tossed both times?

   _____

5. A coin is flipped three times. Which is the probability heads will come up all
   three times?

   A likely   **B** unlikely   **C** impossible   **D** certain

6. **Writing to Explain** If a coin is flipped, and the spinner is
   spun, how many total possible outcomes are there? Explain.

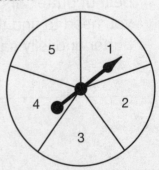

Writing Probability as a Fraction

Karina is playing a game with a number cube labeled 1, 3, 4, 5, 6, and 9.

1. How many outcomes are possible? _____

2. What is the probability that Karina will roll a 6? _____

3. What is the probability that she will roll an odd number? _____

4. What is the probability that she will roll an even number? _____

5. What is the probability that she will roll a number divisible by 3? _____

6. What is the probability that she will roll a two-digit number? _____

7. What is the probability that she will roll a number other than 1? _____

Circle the correct letter for each answer.

8. Lauren spins a spinner that is equally divided into 8 sections. Each section is numbered 1 through 8. What is the probability she will not spin an 8?

A $\frac{1}{8}$

B $\frac{3}{8}$

C $\frac{1}{2}$

D $\frac{7}{8}$

9. You toss a number cube labeled 1 through 6. What is the probability you will toss a number greater than 1?

A $\frac{5}{6}$

B $\frac{4}{6}$

C $\frac{2}{6}$

D $\frac{1}{6}$

10. Writing to Explain The probability of rolling a 3 on a number cube is $\frac{1}{2}$. How many faces on the cube have a 3?

_____

Problem Solving:
Use Reasoning

Solve each problem. Write the answer in a complete sentence.

1. There are 5 students waiting at the bus stop: Donald, Mimi, Wendy, Lance, and Clair. Their ages are 13, 12, 10, 9, and 8. Donald is the oldest and Wendy is the youngest. Lance is 10. Clair is older than Mimi. How old is Mimi?

_____

2. Four friends brought sandwiches to a picnic. Who brought the turkey sandwich?

	Turkey	Tuna	Peanut Butter and Jelly	Roast Beef
Derek		Y		
Ashley				
Trisha			N	
Steve				Y

3. Jud is thinking of a prime number that is not even. Which number could he be thinking of?

A 0   **B** 2   **C** 5   **D** 9

4. Writing to Explain Ingrid lives on either Milton Street or Byron Street. Katie lives on either Byron Street or Whitman Street. Katie does not live on the same street as Ingrid. If Ingrid lives on Milton Street, can Katie live on Byron Street? Why or why not?

_____

_____

_____